D1535074

TechnoSelling

How to Use Today's Technology to Increase Your Sales

TechnoSelling

How to Use Today's Technology to Increase Your Sales

by

Ed Callaghan and Peter W. Nauert

Lone Star Publishing
2300 Highland Village Rd., Suite 320
Highland Village, TX 75067

Although the authors and publisher have made every effort to ensure the accuracy and completeness of information and sources contained in this book, we assume no responsibility for errors, inaccuracies, omissions, or any inconsistency herein. Any slights of people, places, or organizations are unintentional. Every attempt was made to find and acknowledge the correct source of information in this book. However, we admit to being human and making mistakes. If we have overlooked or incorrectly credited a product or source, we apologize. We are not in any way endorsing the products mentioned in this book or intentionally leaving out any products. We are only trying to share what we found out. If we left out your product or service it's probably because we didn't know about it.

ISBN 0-9645225-0-0

LCCN 95-75538

First printing 1995

Editing, design, typesetting, and printing services provided by About Books, Inc., 425 Cedar Street, Buena Vista, CO 81211, 800 548-1876.

Attention: Corporations, Universities, Colleges, and Professional Organizations: Quantity discounts are available on bulk purchases of this book for educational purposes or fund raising. Special books or book excerpts can also be created to fit specific needs. For information, please contact our Lone Star Publishing, 2300 Highland Village Rd., Suite 320, Highland Village, TX 75067, or call 800 896-9500.

Special Thanks

A word of appreciation to Georglyn Estruth Rosenfeld, contributing editor for *TechnoSelling*, who collaborated with us on the research and writing process and helped us refine our thoughts and ideas.

Table of Contents

Preface

"If we did business with the consumer of the '90s the same way we did business with the consumer of the '80s, we'd be out of business in 2000."

—Joseph Antonini, Chairman
K-mart Corporation

Change is always coming and change is always here. The way we do business today has changed, and continues to change, at exponential speed. How these changes affect our careers and our lives is important for us to understand and we must take a proactive stance toward those coming changes. We must accept change as a challenge and welcome the opportunities it brings with it. We must be on the cutting edge of technology or our customers and our competitors will pass us by and we will forever be playing catch-up. Successful business executives and salespeople need to know where technology is heading and how to harness that technology. In this book we are emphasizing how technology is changing the way we sell today and how we will be selling in the future. It's going to be very different.

Whether you're in sales, marketing, or management; a customer, entrepreneur, or corporate CEO; this book has something to offer you. The collaboration of two CEOs has resulted in this guidebook to help you leverage current and future technology to build your sales. Peter Nauert is the chairman of the board of Pioneer Financial Services, and oversees several very large insurance companies. He is a salesman at heart and understands how both salespeople and executives feel about today's marketplace and the effect of technology on that same marketplace.

Ed Callaghan is the president of National Training Corporation and has been training salespeople and sales managers for over twenty-five years. Ed has been teaching and still teaches the traditional sales skills and trains over fifteen hundred of Peter Nauert's salespeople each year.

Peter is known as the visionary and futurist of this team, always on the cutting edge of new ideas and markets, seizing opportunities before others know they exist. We hope this combination provides the reader with a new perspective on our changing sales world.

This book is written to help you raise your level of awareness about new technology and how to use that knowledge to improve your bottom line. The authors wish to help those who hate or don't understand current technology without boring the gadget lovers and techno-experts.

Part I

How Technology Is Changing the Selling Environment

Chapter 1

Will Your Company or Career Be Uprooted By the Forces of Technology?

"Survival for any species depends on the ability to come to terms with the prevailing change agent, whether it's a drought that destroys crops or a chain saw that cuts down the rain forest. The most powerful change agent we have is technology."

—Daniel Burrus[1]

In the biological world, plants and animals become extinct when they are unable to adapt to drastic change or relocate to a less hostile environment. Businesses and salespeople also face extinction if they can't adjust to the rapid changes brought about by technology.

Information technology changed the world. Global competition and technology turned many businesses and sometimes entire industries upside down. Old style, management-heavy corporations were toppled when high-tech entrepreneurs took a large share of their market. During the '80s, 230 companies (46 percent) disappeared from the Fortune 500 list. Blue chip companies fell off the list and were replaced by previously unknown companies that utilized today's information technology. Possibly the companies that didn't survive didn't have the foresight to recognize that the changes around them threatened their survival. How can we learn from their mistakes? Even the strongest business entrepreneurs, salespeople, corporate executives, and marketers must become familiar with existing technology, learn to identify trends, and accept and embrace change—or consumers will pass them by.

This is an era in which two young men without college educations could create a computer in their garage, causing a major corporation to lose its 60 percent share of the world computer market. Steven Wozniak and Steve Jobs created a personal computer and a $100 billion market with their innovative manufacturing and sales techniques, taking a hard bite out of IBM's mainframe business.

In this environment, computer technology wreaked havoc on a 200-year-old publishing company with sales of $650 million and a brand name recognized all over the world. CD-ROM technology has dealt a near fatal blow to *Encyclopedia Britannica* just the way the fax machine took the life of Western Union's telegraph service.

Many consumers prefer to pay between $100 and $400 for a CD-ROM encyclopedia and have it include sound, graphics, and video on their computer monitors rather than pay *Encyclopedia Britannica* $1500 for a set of books that weigh 118 pounds and takes up nearly five feet of shelf space.

Cavett Robert, a well-known speaker and sales trainer, often says, "The old oaken bucket company went out of business because they thought they were in the bucket business." Unfortunately, that is true of many companies. Sometimes they forget what they sell and who their market is.

Encyclopedia Britannica apparently thought they were in the book business when they were actually in the information business. Britannica once owned Compton's encyclopedias and when CD technology came along they developed Compton's on CD-ROM, introduced it in 1990, and it became an instant hit. So successful, in fact, that they thought it would be a good source of cash to bolster their book division, and sold Compton's to Chicago's Tribune Company for $57 million. Unfortunately, they also agreed not to compete with a multimedia version of *Encyclopedia Britannica* for two years.

Owned by a charitable foundation, the Britannica Corporation earned more than $40 million after tax in 1990, on sales of $650 million. According to the foundation's tax report, it lost $12 million in 1991 and also suffered a loss in 1992.[2]

Embracing CD technology would have changed the nature of Britannica's hard sale, the sales force, and the commission. Apparently they hoped if they ignored it, technology wouldn't affect them. They were wrong. In 1992 Britannica had twenty-three hundred active sales reps who sold encyclopedias in homes for a $300 commission. At the beginning of 1994 Britannica had fewer than eleven hundred sales reps. Now Britannica advertises their books with an insert in cable TV bills and offers a group discount for cable TV subscribers. Times have changed. Encyclopedias are sold, compact disks are bought.

Other publishers saw the opportunity in CD-ROMs, however, and jumped on board to supply their product to the estimated 16 million American homes predicted to own computer CD drives by the end of 1994.

In 1880 when Thomas Edison invented the phonograph, he remarked to his assistant Sam Insull, "The phonograph . . . is not of any commercial value." Then it was decided that its future was mainly to teach foreign languages. One hundred years later the phonograph is not of much commercial value, but until the invention of CD players billions of phonographs were sold.

When Tower Records named their store, if anyone told them that thanks to a new technology in a few years people would no longer be buying records, they would have laughed. Their name is still shown in the 1995 phone book as "Tower Records," but how many records do you suppose they sold in 1995? Do they still even carry records? Is there a recycling center or music graveyard for vast collections of obsolete records? CDs changed the music, publishing, and computer industries and will continue to change and create other companies as new applications emerge.

If you're not in the music or book business, you might think CD-ROM technology doesn't affect you. Don't be too sure. Not only is it one of the fastest growing industries in the world, but new applications and uses are being found for it every day. (Chapter 6 gives an overview of how companies are using CD-ROM technology.)

CD-ROMs are not the only example of technology changing the way we live and the way companies do business. A similar occurrence happened to the watch industry. In 1968, the Swiss had more than 65 percent of the world watch market and 80 percent of the profits. Yet, by 1980, their market share had dropped to less than 10 percent. That translated into a loss of fifty thousand jobs, or 80 percent of the industry work force. Japan, meanwhile, had risen from less than 1 percent of the market in 1968 to 33 percent by 1980.[3]

Why? The Japanese embraced the new technology, the electronic quartz watch, which the Swiss had rejected. Would you be familiar with Casio watches today if they had tried to compete with the jeweled mechanisms made by the Swiss? The Japanese listened to the winds of change and harnessed their power. How about you? Are you listening to the breeze outside your window?

In *Reengineering the Corporation*, authors Hammer and Champy state:

> The reality that organizations have to confront, however, is that the old ways of doing business . . . simply don't work anymore. Suddenly, the world is a different place . . . In today's environment, nothing is constant or predictable—not market growth, customer demand, product life cycles, the rate of technological change, or the nature of competition. Adam Smith's world and its way of doing business are yesterday's paradigm.[4]

Hammer and Champey list three forces, separately and in combination, driving today's companies deeper and deeper into territory most of their executives and managers find frighteningly unfamiliar. These forces are: customers, competition, and change. Customers now tell suppliers what they want, when they want it, how they want it, and what they will pay. The mass market has broken into pieces, some as small as a single customer. Technology has changed the nature of competition, with the customer frequently setting the standards. Also, thanks to technology and other factors, we are now competing globally.

Change has become both pervasive and persistent. It is the norm. Not only have product and service life cycles diminished, but so has the time available to develop new products and introduce them. Today companies must move fast or they won't be moving at all. The changes that will put a company out of business are those happening outside the light of its current expectations, and that is the source of most change in today's business environment.[5]

Digital technology has created enormous possibilities by combining with other industries such as publishing, banking, or watchmaking. Merging computer technology and publishing created new opportunities and industries for some and caused others to suffer. Converging interactive computing with the telephone and cable TV industries is creating new products, services, and markets that are changing the way we live and shop. Therefore, we must change *what* we sell and the *way* we sell if we don't want to be left stranded by the wayside.

New markets and opportunities are created every day by new technologies. Digital audio and video, wireless communications, videoconferencing, video servers and networks, storage devices, and on-line services provide new ways of working, playing, communicating, and selling.

Creative entrepreneurs, sales, and marketing people need to look at today's technology and the future technology and make applications for their business or create a new business. For example, Daniel and Timothy Price decided to merge computers with voice-processing and telecommunications technology and created the Send-A-Song Corp. in Vienna, Virginia, whereby customers could send popular songs as gifts over the phone. For $9.95 each or $19.95 for three messages, Send-A-Song will call your friends or associates and play a digitized version of one of more than two hundred selections by popular recording artists, plus your recorded personal message. Call Interactive, in Omaha, a joint venture between AT&T and American Express Information Services, processes the orders for Send-A-Song and can handle fifty thousand calls per hour.

Three days before Valentine's Day in 1992, their company was highlighted on the front page of *USA Today's* Life section. More than three thousand calls came in the first day and continued until they had to stop taking orders for Valentine's Day. In 1993 their service was featured on *CNN Headline News* plus numerous radio stations and newspapers. Over sixty thousand orders were processed for Valentine's Day. In 1994 they ran a large ad in the *Wall Street Journal* claiming Send-A-Song "is the best way ever to express your love." A song list was included in the ad listing seventeen love songs ranging from "I Just Called To Say I Love You," by Stevie Wonder to "How Sweet It Is (To Be Loved By You)" by James Taylor.

Daniel and Timothy Price capitalized on technology that didn't exist a few years ago, combined it with a threefold marketing plan and have projected revenues of $56 million for 1995. If you want to see how this innovative service works, call 800 SEND-A-SONG.[6]

Why do you need to know about technology?

A decade ago 124,000 fax machines were in use in this country. The number now exceeds 11 million. Ten years ago there were 16.5 million personal computers in this country. Now it's more than 50 million. Another 16 million will be sold this year. About 13 million Americans have access to on-line information. A new network is connected to the Internet every ten minutes.[7] Cellular phone subscribers in the United States have jumped from zero in 1983 to 16 million in 1993.

When used correctly, a cellular phone, a fax machine, voice-mail, and a computer with a modem and E-mail capabilities are a salesperson's umbilical cord to the world—allowing you to stay in touch and work wherever you are. If your customers are trying to reach you and you aren't wired, or continue to be a computer laggard, they will call your closest competitor who is wired. Joseph Wiencko, manager of advanced network systems at Virginia Tech, predicts that at some point early in the twenty-first century one-third to one-half of our GNP will be conducted over the information superhighway. The question is, how do you get from here to there? The answer, simply, is that you either get connected or you get left out.[8]

Whether you are part of a billion-dollar corporation or a one-person entrepreneur managing your own sales territory, technology has something to offer you. Millions of consumers are awaiting your innovative ideas. You're not going to reach them all, but why not carve out a market niche and concentrate on them? It is our hope that you will apply some of the ideas in this book to create a new business or drastically change and improve your existing products, services, and sales.

All the equipment, products, and services we discuss in this book can be used to complement face-to-face selling. Some of the tools will replace personal contact—and in that sense could become your competitor—if you don't learn ways to use them to your advantage.

A wired Willy Loman?

Technology has created and destroyed businesses as well as careers. What will it do to selling as a career? Already it has a significant impact on the way we sell. Those who embrace technology and use it to their advantage will do well in sales. Those who don't utilize existing technology in order to improve their own business and help solve customers' problems will be pushed aside by competitors who do.

According to Majorie Weiss, publisher of *Selling* magazine, "The rate at which salespeople embrace new technologies will accelerate in the next few years, as today's reluctant adopters become tomorrow's enthusiastic proponents."

We will be the first to admit that some customers dislike technology as much as some salespeople. In fact, you may be one of those individuals who has never spent even a nanosecond in front of a computer. Some customers in today's market and the market of the future will prefer high-touch over high-tech. We represent both sides of the continuum and realize we need to achieve a balance between the two to meet your customers' needs. Computers can augment and assist with the personal touch, not replace it all of the time. High-tech makes it possible for you to give personalized high-touch service to a greater number of customers.

How does this affect you?

Selling is being redefined by technology. Some products and services will be affected more than others. Many customers prefer personal contact and will resist electronic shopping. All customers, however, will appreciate the extra convenience and service you can offer them when you use the new tools.

Technology has changed the way we live, work, shop, what we buy, and how we buy it. Therefore, it has to change the way we sell and what we sell, or we will find ourselves watching the parade of consumers pass us by. The old ways don't work anymore. Both the medium and the delivery systems have changed. In many cases the delivery has become the product. Technology has given us new ways to identify our customers, advertise, market, and sell our changing products.

As our attitudes, values, and beliefs change, new trends are emerging and society itself changes. Salespeople, marketers, business executives, and entrepreneurs need to be aware of these changes and incorporate them into the way they do business.

For years marketing geniuses have said, "If you build a better mousetrap the world will beat a path to your door." In today's market that statement is not true—if in fact it ever was true. We must use technology to locate the customer's door and then enter it through an information highway off-ramp. But before you try to sell the mousetrap, make sure the mouse isn't already dead. Innovative technology is never enough by itself, it must have a purpose. Real life applications to the market must be utilized to identify, reach, and inform the potential customer.

According to George Colombo, author of *Sales Force Automation*, "Two new technologies will create massive changes in the way salespeople work—personal digital assistants and wireless communications." And, he says, "Those two technologies will work together to put information at the fingertips of salespeople instantly and effortlessly—anytime, anywhere."[9]

What can you do with this knowledge?

One of the benefits of sales automation is the way it expedites and expands communications with your customers, your home office, other salespeople, and anyone else on Internet E-mail. SMCS, a sales automation system marketed by GE Information Services of Rockville, Maryland, allows salespeople to access electronic bulletin boards, set up a personalized electronic news-clipping service, and maintain an on-line relational database for such functions as lead tracking, call reporting, order entry, and tickler file notification—all for the price of a local phone call.

In order to be cost-effective, technology must be utilized in ways that will assist the salespeople, the home office, and the marketing and sales managers, as well as the customer. For example, buying a computer and just using it for a day-timer or prospecting and follow-up system is not utilizing it to its full advantage. Technology must serve a purpose. Utilize it by accessing, managing, and using information to make better, faster, more efficient decisions, build relationships with customers, and increase sales. If a computer isn't used to interact with other people and gather information, it really isn't anything more than a $3,000 calendar and organizer.

As you read this book and see how other companies and salespeople are using technology, ask yourself how you can use technology to:

- Build your customer base
- Identify your market with demographic software
- Reach your market by targeting a specific marketing niche
- Meet customers' needs
- Augment your communication with customers on a customized, individualized basis
- Make applications for others in the market
- Obtain more information faster
- Make a dynamic presentation on your laptop computer
- Keep your focus on selling and less on paperwork
- Communicate with other salespeople in the field
- Become a desktop marketer
- Conquer new territories with demographic software
- Tap on-line data banks
- Make your records accessible when you are out
- Lower your costs by cutting back on overhead, personnel, travel expenses, equipment
- Join forces with another business or industry to create a new product, delivery system, or service

- Reinvent yourself by reorganizing your systems, techniques, territory, or other aspects of your business
- Retain personal information about customers
- Flatter customers by knowing and remembering their preferences and personal data
- Provide better customer service
- Cultivate relationship selling
- Manage your time better
- Sell the right product to the right customer
- Assist in identifying trends and patterns

Will technology replace salespeople?

In some areas, yes. In most areas, no. The role of all salespeople has drastically changed, however, and will continue to change. The new role will include information agent, teacher, educator, and community resource. According to Alice LaPlante:

> . . . the role of the salesperson will change dramatically as technology advances. Alternative distribution channels such as electronic catalogs will certainly flourish. Customer relationships may evolve as well—to the point where sales reps may never actually meet their customers face to face. Electronic links will probably do just fine, especially if they include video conferencing, E-mail hookups or frequent telephone conversations. Expect customers' tolerance for slow information and delayed shipments to keep dropping like a stone.[10]

Andy Kessler irritated a lot of *Forbes* readers when he said, "Fire your sales force, and empower your customer." Kessler recommends that companies figure out what they really sell and then harness the interactivity and interconnectivity inside their enterprise to facilitate sales outside the enterprise. He continues:

> Building your future in a global economy by cutting costs to tick up productivity is only half the equation. You'll still need to ratchet up output—sell more products and services.

One way to do this is to take advantage of the 50 million networked PCs that already exist on white-collar desktops and achieve both productivity and growth.[11]

Denying the trend to eliminate salespeople, agents, and distributors and replacing them with technology that empowers the customers could be a fatal mistake. Customers will be empowered by making them the sales force. By creating direct sales channels through internal networks and client/server applications the cost per sale will be much lower than existing sales channels. Virtual corporations access and communicate directly with their customers.

Companies are empowering both their customers and their salespeople through advancements in data communications giving them anytime, anywhere communications and access to numerous data bases. Salespeople are still valuable assets in the selling equation, but their role will change to information agent, problem solver, and facilitator. Each visit will provide answers and seek solutions.

Although technology has forever changed the way we communicate with our customers and the speed and amount of information we can access, human relations will always be important. It will be even more so in the future as customers want long-term relationships with salespeople who understand their situation. However, customers will only want to deal with salespeople who use today's technology.

Information agents

Knowledge is power which can be used or abused. Those with the most information will have the most power. When the same people who sell the product provide the information, it may be construed as biased by some people. In the future, information will be provided for a fee by those who are independent of the manufacturers or salespeople. Specialists will be utilized to generate, gather, organize, synthesize, transform, make applications, and dispense information obtained from customers, competitors, employees, management, and market research.

Information is a commodity for many industries and will be dispensed via packaging, TV, special studies and consumer reports. The success of the company will depend upon how accurate the information is and how fast it is utilized or acted upon.

Information packaging offers a wide variety of formats for new products and services. Choose between print, digital, on-line, interactive CDs, video, and multimedia. We already have information packages available on CD-ROM catalogs, on-line services, computer data bases, and "900" numbers. When you repackage information in new ways, you create new users, new markets and new revenue. Computer knowledge will create powerful opportunities for entrepreneurs who want to offer new products and services which were not possible before computer technology.

Information agents will turn salespeople into order takers in some industries. In other industries, salespeople will become information agents and will get paid whether or not they take the order. Already, close to one-third of IBM's salespeople have traded in quotas for billable hours as they transform themselves into the newest breed of salesperson: the consultant.[12]

Team selling

A team of experts incorporating all aspects of research, development, production, marketing, inventory, shipping, and sales will work with the customers to assist them with their business. More than one salesperson will work on each account with salespeople sharing in the profits as a group or billing for their time as consultants.

For hundreds of tasks, corporations will turn to teams of consultants and independent contractors who specialize more and more narrowly as markets globalize and technologies differentiate. Globalization demands independent specialists, especially in the area of information technology.

Elimination of the middleman

Many consumers now go directly to the manufacturer for products, eliminating the middleman. Consumer magazines rate computers with such detail that customers base their decision on published, unbiased information and frequently buy directly from the manufacturer rather than a consumer electronics store.

Numerous insurance companies already offer insurance without going through insurance agents. A Tampa, Florida company, Fee for Service Inc., offers "Low load" insurance products with minimum overhead costs for policies because no sales commission is paid. This is done through their Whole Insurance Network (WIN). Potential customers report their age, what type of policy they want, the amount of coverage they need, and whether or not they smoke. WIN will send the customer free quotes, application forms, illustrations of possible future value, and some information about the company for no charge. Also, if the customer has received a new policy proposal from an insurance agent, WIN will evaluate it to see if they can beat the price. Call WIN at 800 808-5810 or fax them at 800 424-0909.[13]

Discount brokers Charles Schwab and Fidelity Investment make it easy for customers to trade stocks, options, warrants, and mutual funds by computer or touch-tone phones. At Schwab about 20 percent of transactions are done without a broker. The brokers sell Fox and StreetSmart software which enables customers to hook into databases and conduct their own research.[14] Many consumers are also buying stock directly from the company rather than going through a stock broker.

Information technology is the great equalizer

In the past, only large companies could afford the latest technology. Now, however, individual salespeople, entrepreneurs, and small businesses on limited budgets can afford to utilize today's technology. This is not only because prices have dropped drastically, but because so much is available on a shared services basis, on-line, or for a per-use charge.

Prototypes already exist for all the new technological products that will be on the market in the next three years. By finding out about them and thinking of ways to utilize them, you'll have a jump on your competitors. Think about ways you can use technology to improve your customer service and help your clients in the future.

"By not focusing on the customer's future needs, an education system or a business dooms itself—and the customer in many cases—to failure," according to Daniel Burrus. "Those future needs are not going to be the same as current or past needs, thanks to technological changes. By looking at the future through the customer's eyes, we can see our own future more clearly."[15]

Stop the world. You want to get off?

You might be saying, "I sell, I don't use computers." Many salespeople are stuck in a technological time warp and have no interest in learning about the ways technology is changing the way we sell and work.

You have a choice. You can choose to live in the past and watch as your competitors walk away with your customers. Or you can choose to start desensitizing yourself to your technophobia and begin using some of the tools of technology in your sales and marketing career.

Throughout this book we will be your tour guides for existing and coming technologies to assist you in thinking of ways you and your customers can profit from them. Apply these technologies to your products and businesses as well as your customers'. Know more about your customers' products and markets than they do. Help them find ways to do things they didn't know were possible. We want to help you be on the cutting edge, a visionary rather than a traditionalist. Start using these technologies in innovative ways. Don't just wait until your competitors use them, then try to catch up. Start learning now!

Successful businesses in the future will be those companies and entrepreneurs who capitalize on new technology and apply it to their existing products and services, or converge with another company or industry to create a new business or service based on a new delivery system.

Technology is the prevailing change agent. You must come to terms with it or your competitors will decimate your business—like the drought that destroys crops or the chain saw that cuts down the rain forest. Use the tools of technology to build your business and your career—before others build theirs at your expense.

Chapter 2

Trends That Are Changing
the Marketplace

"You can trust a crystal ball about as far as you can throw it."
—Faith Popcorn[1]

In 1899 Commissioner Duell of the U.S. Patent Office recommended the office be closed down because "everything that can be invented has been invented." According to Marvin J. Cetron, president and founder of Forecasting International, Ltd., all the technological knowledge we work with today will represent only 1 percent of the knowledge that will be available in 2050.

New information technologies are generating enormous productivity gains in manufacturing, marketing, retailing, and services. Businesses are reengineering to adapt to the changes, just as salespeople need to adapt to maintain a competitive advantage. Products will be brought to the market faster and become obsolete before competitors can do any damage.

Some of these new technologies are already in place and many are recognizable to us all. For example, electronic point-of-purchase data collection has revolutionized retailing. Electronic Data Interchange (EDI), Universal Product Codes (UPC), and Computerized Price Lookup (PLU) will continue to gain in popularity since they make it so easy to computerize sales and inventory information down to the level of the individual transaction. EDI makes it possible for sellers to immediately transmit this information to others throughout the distribution process, using a combination of computers and telecommunications.

With EDI, chain headquarters can know on a daily basis exactly what is selling in every store. Vendors can order supplies and pay bills from outside suppliers and central warehouses without the slowness and cost of manual systems. Almost every major manufacturer and retailer in the United States today is using EDI. John Roach, chief executive officer of the Tandy Corporation says: "Every morning I know how many products by model, by price, by gross margin were sold the previous day."[2]

Some of the technologies that we are not addressing in this book but which will have a direct impact on the marketplace and customer service include computer-aided design, voice recognition, advanced fiber optics, flash and graphics technology, and virtual reality.

The virtual corporation

"Virtual" means being in effect but not in form or appearance. A "virtual" corporation means that its products are the same as any other corporation of its kind, but it does not look like or act as a traditional business. Frequently referred to as "virtual corporations," they seem to exist any time and any place they are needed, outsourcing just about everything in the pursuit of eternal flexibility, low overhead, and the leading edge.

Virtual corporations are built around tasks, information networks, flexible working conditions, and people with entrepreneurial attitudes, rather than meaningless tasks, organizational charts, and strictly enforced hours at the office. For example, in an on-going attempt to reengineer, Levi Strauss recently streamlined their policy manual from seven hundred pages to fifty.

Today's trend toward low-overhead, high-tech businesses—with an entirely flexible workforce spread out all over the country, communicating by wireless modem—is something like we might have seen on *Mission Impossible* thirty years ago. Businesses may operate out of a large building in a major metropolitan area or in someone's home on lakefront property. E-mail, on-line networks, wireless modems, fax machines, overnight mail, laptop and palmtop computers, video-conferencing, and telecommuting make it all possible.

Whether we call them "virtual" or "reengineered," they will be lean and flexible, rather than top-heavy, allowing employees to work on projects wherever they are, rather than just putting in time at the office.

Deregulation

Due to a Federal Communications Commission ruling in 1992, restrictions were lifted, allowing telephone companies to carry other types of signals. A variety of new delivery systems will arrive with deregulation. Cable TV companies, telephone companies, fiber-optic network providers, and mobile telephone systems will form alliance or partnership relationships. Manufacturers serving these companies will sell to each other's customers. Television signals may soon be transmitted over telephone wires.

Cable TV companies may offer phone service. Fiber-optic networks may replace both and be the delivery system of the future. Coaxial wire is already in wide use and technological advances enable it to transmit fax or video at the same time as voice.

Partnering and strategic alliances

Partnering is a strategic new alternative to whether or not to "in-house" or "outsource" the job. Partnering builds close relationships with subcontractors and suppliers to achieve higher productivity and quality.

Strategic alliances focus primarily on product or market innovation. They create relationships with competitors or companies in related industries where both parties pool resources, investment, and risk.

According to Doug Wilson of the Wilson Consulting Group in Newport Beach, California, success in partnering is a precursor to successful strategic alliances. Working as a team with suppliers to improve current products is one of the best ways to learn how to manage complex alliances. Wherever there is a supplier/customer relationship, there is a place for partnering.

Formerly adversarial relationships will turn into cooperative partnerships. Cable TV operators will team up with mobile phone systems or alternative fiber-optic network providers. Suppliers and customers will share information and expertise to form an alliance against global competitors. Many start-up companies search for strategic alliances with companies around the world to market their technologies.

Motorola sends its suppliers through Motorola University in Mesa, Arizona so they can share their values and teach their Total Quality Management techniques. Suppliers are required to take courses in customer satisfaction and are even given report cards.

The end result of these partnerships will be products getting to market faster for a lower cost. Competitive bidding will be out in some industries. Alliance partnerships will be in. Commitments between corporations will replace sales agreements between salespeople and purchasing agents.

Mass customization

Technology brought us the assembly line and mass production around the turn of the century. Now new information technology—the silicon chip—has taken us a step further and given us the ability to mass-produce customized goods.

Mass customization—a "one person/one product" approach to sales—is becoming a customer service trend in products and services ranging from automobiles and bicycles to computers, financial services, office supplies, and video stores. Customers now want it the way they want it, when they want it, and at a price they can afford. By blending humans and machines, high-tech, low-tech, and mid-tech service, and utilizing the speed, capacity, and utility of information and telecommunications technologies, customers can have variety at a competitive price. Using computer integrated manufacturing, companies link production, sales, design, finance, and operations into a single system that is fast, responsive, and flexible.

At Bally Engineered Structures in Bally, Pennsylvania, salesmen, engineers, and operations personnel can tap into a PC network anchored by a midrange file server to tinker with product specifications. All the company's regional offices are integrated via computer. An outside salesperson uses a laptop computer to dial into the system via modem and design a product to his specifications. These flow through to the MRP files, meaning Material Requirements Planning, or computerized scheduling of the factory floor. Specifics in the files determine steps in the production process. The finished product is compared with a model constructed through computer-aided design, and a drawing is sent to the customer.

Other technologies that support customization include computer numerical control, computer-aided design, material requirements planning, and computer-aided manufacturing. According to John Nichols of Illinois Tool Works, "Customers want more variety . . . You have to interface with the customer and use all the toys at your disposal . . . to satisfy their needs . . . the issue is pushing technology down to the front lines and passing on benefits to customers."[3]

No-haggle, one-price policy

Industries that historically have negotiated price are now adopting a one-price selling strategy. A study by J.D. Power and Associates found that the number of dealers offering a one-price selling strategy increased by 71 percent in one year and that 15 percent of all automobile dealers would offer a one-price policy in 1993. According to the report, this no-haggle policy has boosted sales, increased dealers' profits and improved customer satisfaction.[4]

Finding the New Consumer

Demographics and segmentation

Rather than being a melting pot, it seems the United States has fragmented into scores of distinct subcultures, each with unique tastes and yearnings of the sort that previously distinguished broad social classes. Diversity is the norm, rather than conformity. Different ethnic groups are clinging to and celebrating their cultural heritage rather than adopting those of the majority.

21

With our class structure now so fragmented, advertisers are forced to home in ever more closely on specific targets. "You've got to use a rifle instead of a shotgun," says Malcolm MacDougall, chief creative officer at Ally & Gargano in Manhattan. Advertisers must take into account the fact that tastes of classes and sub-groups are shifting more rapidly now than decades ago.[5]

Target marketing to a segment of one

Individuals are more important in marketing than groups. Target marketing, personalization, and custom publishing are delivering information in smaller, more selective, more personal "bites." When the right information reaches the right person, the result is a greater, higher-quality response and a stronger, more profitable relationship with your audience.

Geographic Information Systems (GIS) link maps with other software and provide geodemographic network databases that run on PCs and hook into global positioning systems (GPS). Sales and marketing execs are now empowered with demographic and geographic information which when combined, greatly increases their knowledge of a specific area's potential for promotions, sales, and income.

Technology has changed the way we identify customers. Sophisticated, easily accessible, and relatively inexpensive databases contain an incredible amount of information regarding what people buy, where they are located, age, income level, ethnic background, etc. These massive customer databases make it possible to track and communicate with individual customers like never before. Successful interaction between people and systems makes it possible to call up a customer's purchase history on a computer terminal and avoid entering all new data.

These databases also give businesses the opportunity to market new products based on the customer's history and response to toll-free numbers in advertisements. Some companies use their database information for a personalized portfolio presentation to a customer. For example, Merrill Lynch introduced a new investment product by sending its customers a personalized analysis of their portfolios that showed what their returns would be if they were to invest in the new product.

Citicorp has tracked the supermarket-shopping habits of 50 million households. They can identify by name and address which households are brand loyal and which are switchers. They can tell you which households use your products and which ones use your competitors' products.[6]

It's a small, small world

International markets are more easily accessible, as the U.S. economy becomes integrated with the international economy and the potential for new audiences grows larger. Tariffs and other trade barriers are falling. The day after the North American Free Trade Agreement (NAFTA) passed, businesses that had been struggling for years signed contracts. Salespeople were no longer detained at Canadian border gates. Many U.S. companies will now be able to compete by utilizing lower-cost manufacturing sites in Mexico. An estimated 39 percent of the parts used in products assembled in the United States are produced in other countries.

International capital markets are also more easily accessible now. We're not just talking about North America, Japan, and Europe. How about Eastern Europe, Latin America, and the Pacific Rim? In the book the *Third Century—America's Resurgence in the Asian Era*, author Joel Kotkin states, "The face of business itself will become increasingly Asian and nonwhite." He predicts that in 1995 trade across the Pacific Ocean will be twice the trade across the Atlantic Ocean.

Gunilla Broadbent, senior vice president at Starch INRA Hooper, a marketing research firm, suggests that invaluable international business marketing perceptions and trends should be tracked by country. For example, Americans' perceptions of Japanese and German cars are that they are of higher quality.

Consumers around the world are demanding higher quality in products and services. Mass media have educated consumers worldwide about the best of everything, and advances in retailing have made it available. According to Peter Kennedy of the Futures Group in Glastonbury, Connecticut, "The poorest slums of Calcutta are home to 70,000 VCRs. In Mexico, homes with color televisions outnumber those with running water."[7]

Thanks to advances in telecommunications, computer networks, and cable-TV home-shopping channels, consumers are no longer geographically undesirable. They want and need your products and services. Your competition might already be importers. Are you giving them competition in their countries?

Both civilian and government buyers will be able to order from any supplier due to the acceptance of global industrial standards—for building materials, fasteners, even factory machinery—rather than only from those with whom they have established relationships. Futurist Marvin J. Cetron states that the acceptance of global standards is one of the most important industrial trends now operating.[8]

Has this strategic entry into global markets had any effect on your business? Will it in the future? Are you creating new ways to use existing information to explore new markets and to generate additional revenue streams for your company?

How We Service and Communicate with Our Customers

The new consumer

The power balance has shifted from marketers to consumers. Part of this power is knowledge. Information technology has given consumers more control over when, where, and how they buy. Independent information sources will replace mass media as a source of information and empower the consumer to access unbiased knowledge. "As the twenty-first century progresses, the consumer's growing information power is bound to transform the marketplace," says James H. Snider, co-author of *Future Shop*. "As always, the businesses that survive will be the ones willing and able to adapt to the consumer's changing needs and behavior."[9]

Fortune magazine recently reported, "The customer isn't king anymore. The customer is dictator . . . whether you sell 100 million dollar planes or 79-cent pens, your buyers have changed enormously in the past few years. Their demands are lengthening; their patience is shrinking. Epochal shifts in the global economy have given them a sultan's power to command exactly what they want, the way they want it, when they want it, at a price that will make you weep. You'll either provide it or vaporize."[10]

Consumers are demanding and getting more information about products—ingredients, fat content, calories from fat, unit pricing, warning labels, etc.—making them more informed buyers. Much of their strength comes from the revolution in information technology. On-line data bases connect buyers to worldwide companies with information about product attributes and prices from every supplier.

When management gives up control and empowers, rather than degrades, their workers and customers, they utilize their vast knowledge for the benefit of the company. In the near future we will see downsizing, restructuring, reorganizing, and closer relationships and/or partnerships formed between customers and suppliers. Effective salespeople will learn about their customers' businesses, needs, and wants and will be problem solvers and specialists rather than order takers. Proctor & Gamble has "business crusaders" who bring their expertise to their counterparts on the Wal-Mart team, whether it's shipping, inventory control, merchandising, or sales. They try to know as much about Wal-Mart's business in their product categories as their counterparts do.

Personalized communications

We now communicate with customers through "800" numbers, video-conferencing, PDAs, fax machines, voice mail, local area networks, multimedia systems, network integration, graphical user interfaces, client/server systems, and electronic data interchange (EDI). We also have computer sorting and storing and forwarding of individualized communications into video mailboxes and electronic bulletin boards. In the future this will become more sophisticated and be available at a lower cost.

Many companies are giving customers direct, on-line access to their computerized ordering and inventory systems. The order may go directly from the customer to the shop floor, and even into the supplier's automated production equipment. Some companies will no longer deal with suppliers who cannot provide this access.

Anytime, anywhere communications

Cellular phones, global satellite communications, computer technology, personal data assistants (PDAs), and wireless modems have given us anytime, anywhere communications giving rise to telecommuting and teleconferencing. Today you can tap into your mainframe office computers, send a fax, or call someone on the other side of the world, twenty-four hours a day, whether you're in your backyard or skiing in Switzerland.

Former Motorola chairman George Fisher proclaimed this the "wireless data decade." The mobile commuting market is attracting every major computer and communications firm in the country. Real-time communications has transformed the way the sales force does business. In the future more companies will find it necessary to empower their field sales force through wireless data communications and mobile computing. Using hand-held computers with a radio frequency modem, sales representatives and their teams can talk to each other anytime, anywhere—and respond to customers immediately. Road warriors will be able to stay connected around the clock, checking inventories, placing orders, and scheduling delivery for customers. United Parcel Service (UPS) has utilized this technology for some time with their PDAs.

The nation's largest wireless data communications network, ARDIS, was founded by IBM and Motorola. Through ARDIS, mobile workers can access information from their company's host computer from almost anywhere. In the future, markets will be more clearly defined. A distinction will be made between short, bursty, and interactive data versus continuous information (documents sent via fax machine or E-mail). The personal communicator and mobile office markets will have evolved. Vertical markets, including field service, field sales and transportation, will continue to enjoy the benefits of wireless. Companies will choose network vendors based upon needs, such as where offices are located and how employees communicate. Vendors will specialize in markets based upon these strengths. For example, ARDIS offers high quality in-building coverage.

Booz, Allen & Hamilton, a management consulting firm in New York City, projects by the year 2000 there will be 8.4

million mobile professionals using wireless data communications. Almost 6 million of these will be classified as mobile office workers. Personal communicator and organization users will comprise 2.5 million.

Where Goods Are Sold

The new retailer

Thirty-two percent of Americans shop at malls less frequently now than they did a year ago, according to the Maritz AmeriPoll, conducted by Maritz Marketing Research of Fenton, Missouri. Only 14 percent shop at malls more frequently. "If this trend affects overall sales, retailers and marketers could be forced to increase promotions," suggests Maritz. "More advertising, merchandise discounts, and other activities may be necessary to ensure growth."[11]

Other surveys validate this trend. According to the 1993 Fall Retail Satisfaction Index, only 46 percent of customers reported department stores as their first preference for men's clothing, compared with 55 percent in the 1992 survey. Forty-five percent reported department stores as their first choice for women's apparel, compared with 54 percent in 1992. Discount department stores were the first choice of 38 percent of respondents for men's clothing, up from 29 percent the previous year. Specialty stores made gains among shoppers for women's apparel, with 22 percent of customers ranking them as their first choice, up from just 14 percent in 1992.[12]

According to a special report by *American Marketplace*, from 1987 to 1992 sales in the off-price retail segment—which includes discount stores, factory outlets, and closeout stores—grew by 65 percent. This double digit annual growth is expected to continue at least through 1996. A study completed by Packaged Facts, a New York market research firm, says the industry will grow from $59.1 billion in sales in 1993 to $97.8 billion by 1997. Off-price retailers are defined as those who offer discounts of 25 percent or more off full price.[13]

Regional malls will be replaced by power centers, a collection of discount centers and one-stop shopping stores. The growth of supercenters is attributed to changing consumer needs. Super-centers allow time-pressed families to accomplish all their shopping needs in one location. "Supercenters are the result of, not the cause of, a changing consumer," said James M. Degen, president of a retail marketing consulting firm. Calling super-centers "retailing's greatest growth concept," Bernard Sosnick, a retail analyst with Oppenheimer & Co., New York, said the United States eventually could have as many as thirty-six hundred hypermarket/supercenters. The Supercenter Industry Overview can be obtained by calling 212 756-5106.[14]

Traditional retailing will be replaced with specialized retailing. Market niches will be fragmented into small segments. Rather than a bell-shaped curve with traditional retail stores in the middle, in the future we will see more of a bimodal distribution with traditional retail stores on the wane. At one end we will see an increase in warehouse, food and price clubs, factory outlets, discount stores, and super stores with one-stop shopping. At the other end of the spectrum we will see more boutiques and specialty stores, but not necessarily for products that can be found in super stores. Possibly they will appeal to specific demographic markets like ethnic groups or specialized interest areas.

The Management Horizons Division of Price Waterhouse presented a report on global retailing which stated in part, " . . . in the 1990s, technology will be the dominant art form in retailing. Failure to develop the most up-to-date systems will relegate a retailer to second-class status and possibly lead to its demise . . . "

If retailers want to compete with home shopping they will need to offer more conveniences, including home delivery.

Home shopping feels good

Home shopping is on the rise for several reasons. Shoppers want convenience and less hassle. Standing in line, tolerating incompetent or rude clerks, and hassling over checks or credit card approvals are some of the reasons many people don't like to go into stores.

According to a survey done by Joe Peritz & Associates, shoppers are most concerned with the time it takes to get in and out of stores. Shoppers placed above-average importance on only five concerns proffered by the surveyors, and three of them involved time:

Most Important—the amount of time required to check out.

Second—the way they were treated in the store.

Third—the amount of time needed to get the things they wanted.

Fourth—the amount of time it took to pay with a credit card.

Fifth—The general atmosphere of the store.[15]

Many companies are capitalizing on this trend. A Lands' End ad during the holidays reads:

Do your Christmas shopping in your PJs. Remember Christmas shopping last year? The traffic, the crowds, the salespeople too harried to help you? It took forever just to get through Gift Wrap. Coming back from the mall, you swore you'd never do that again. Well, here's a little suggestion: this year shop in the Lands' End catalog. It's our 'store,' and it's never, ever crowded. You can browse whenever you feel the urge. And come as you are . . . Call any time, day or night. (Yes, Virginia, we're still friendly at 3 A.M.) . . .

Crime and fear are also changing the way we shop. America's Research Group found one-third of U.S. shoppers are making changes because of fear of crime. They are cutting back on nighttime shopping, carrying less cash, and spending fewer hours in shopping malls. Forty percent of U.S. households are expected to experiment with electronic shopping via TV or computer—for everything from housewares to clothes to groceries—in the next eighteen months. Researcher Watts Wacker of Yankelovich Partners attributes the shift to fear of crime rather than great bargains on the information highway.

Not only is home shopping on the rise, but new ways to do so are continually coming across the wires. We already have print catalogs, newspapers and magazines with "800" numbers on their ads for telephone or fax machine shopping, direct response commercials, home shopping networks, infomercials, video malls, computer and CD-ROM on-line ordering.

CommerceNet, a joint venture involving Apple Computer, Sun Microsystems, and Bank of America, offers home shopping via Internet whereby users can buy computers, scan catalogs and scroll company directories. "We're not sure how it's going to evolve, it could include everything from pizza parlors to real estate," says Steve Harari, president of project manager Enterprise Integration Technologies Corp. The system will use advanced encryption technology to scramble messages and use other methods to ensure orders and credit card numbers are not tampered with by computer hackers.[16]

WSL Marketing of New York found that 25 percent of at-home shoppers have annual household incomes of more than $55,000. Almost all respondents had at least a high school diploma. While the products purchased via television have been limited largely to jewelry, consumers lately have begun to buy a wider variety of products such as clothing, collectibles, housewares, home appliances, beauty products, and consumer electronics—including computers. Impulse shopping was found to be a strong trend among at-home shoppers, with only one in three surveyed actually planning to shop. Three-quarters of at-home shoppers, however, said they planned to shop via television at the same rate or better in the coming year.[17]

Why People Buy

Customers are buying solutions, not products

In the past, we emphasized transaction-based selling. Today we see strong emphasis on relationship-based selling.

Many suppliers are now participating in customers' decisions at a level formerly handled by outside consultants. Both Hewlett-Packard (H-P) and Xerox are closely involved in their customers' work processes. H-P's sales force plays the role of adviser and consultant. For example, with large global customers like Citicorp, they brainstorm about what multi-media applications might be in retail banking's future. Contracts have been reduced from ten to twenty pages to two or three pages for all customers. H-P's computer sales in fiscal 1992 grew 17.5 percent; sales to large global customers grew twice as much.[18]

New change leaders are evolving

In the past, major metropolitan areas like New York and Los Angeles were the centers of new trends and styles which took hold and gradually spread across the nation in a geographical pattern readily predicted and identified by marketers. Young, affluent Yuppies were considered the trendsetters. Now, however, some experts predict that "change leaders" will be the middle-aged population by 2000; and the "youth culture" will be "out."

Today, people who were previously referred to as "nerds" are the trendsetters and early adopters of new products and services based on computer technology. Basically, they are the only ones who initially understood how to use the products. The rest of us become the laggards, waiting until we're sure it's not going to go away before we devote the time and effort to understand what's going on.

Today, information processing, feedback from consumers, media, markets, and manufacturing seem to evolve together. The future will belong to new forms of media and the people who embrace them first. Businesses that understand the relationship between "change leaders" and new media can develop new products for markets before the markets are flooded with competition.[19]

Attitudes and values impact sales

Once again we are seeing a shift in work ethics, attitudes toward money, family values, the importance of health and safety, and the acceptance of personal responsibility. What kind of social statement a corporation makes and its attitude toward the environment often determine whether or not consumers will do business with it.

A survey by the Opinion Research Corporation revealed that over 50 percent of adults say a company's support of cultural activities and its efforts to meet societal obligations are very important factors in forming opinions about that company. Older adults are most likely to say it is very important for a company to have good relations with its home community. But a company's responsiveness to community needs is more important to younger people.[20]

31

Social awareness and community service builds public loyalty and improves a corporation's public image and profitability. If a company is polluting the environment, socially responsible consumers will not want to purchase its products. Consumers may reach for your product over a competitor's because they realize they will be helping the good causes your company supports, as long as they aren't self-serving.

Green products and packaging

In the future, more emphasis will be placed on biodegradable containers and products friendly to the environment. Consumers will resist buying products that are harmful to animals, either in testing or unnecessary or painful slaughter. Environmentalism will be a strong marketing point as companies search for green products and technologies which will address pollution, ozone depletion, saving the rain forest, and more specifically, causes closer to home.

As part of Arm & Hammer's "green is good business policy," it conducts ongoing dialogs with the private, public, and non-profit sectors. According to Bryan Thomlinson, the company's environmental and public policy director, baking soda–based circuit board cleaners, solvent replacements, and graffiti-removal products were a direct result of suggestions from environmentalists. Their green strategy has resulted in $75 million per year in new product sales and incremental increases for existing lines.

Companies will start thinking of waste products as resources. "All waste is lost profit," according to Sandra Woods, public policy manager for Coors Brewing Co. of Golden, Colorado. Coors has made deliberate efforts to spin off businesses fueled by waste products from the brewing process. Spent grain is sold for fertilizer and seed by the newly created Zeagen Company. Aluminum waste and cans collected from consumers are recycled by Coors subsidiary Golden Recycling.[21]

Natural laws are going to become more important as consumers realize they have to abide by them or perish. "The environment will continue as the issue of the nineties," says Chief Oren Lyons, of the Iroquois tribes, " . . . The road to the future is very short. The human being has challenged time. He says: Look at my technology. I have a chain saw and can cut down that black walnut tree in fifteen minutes. It'll take a hundred and fifty years to grow that tree again . . . We won't have wars about communism and capitalism—they'll be about land and natural resources."[22]

Principles that never die

Predicting and understanding trends are necessary for our future survival, but it is also vitally important that we not lose sight of our values. Brian Perkins, Director of Product Management for McNeil Consumer Products Company summed it up this way:

> Trends will come and trends will go, but meeting the needs of your customer, taking care of your employees, and being responsible to the communities in which we live and work are basic values that will never go out of style. They will also lead to long-term gains for any corporation's stockholders. These principles . . . will still be in style in one hundred years.[23]

As the winds of change are blowing they bring with them trends and opportunities for growing profits as well as threats to existing strategies and profits. The more you watch, anticipate, and prepare for the changes, the more you will profit from them.

Chapter 3

If They Build It, These Will Come
(Selling in a High-Tech World)

"Like radio, television, and all new media, the technology is emerging long before the social impact is understood. The real challenge is using technology to entertain, to inform, to sell. That's a matter of trial, error, and inspired creativity."

—Richard Adler

We're all familiar with network and cable television, not to mention video cassette recorders and compact disks. They are part of our world, along with old reliables such as radio and the movies. Amazing, isn't it, what has transpired in just one hundred years? It wasn't that long ago none of these products existed and people were traveling by horse and reading by oil lamps. Today, 60 percent of households with televisions have cable TV. The proportion will reach 87 percent by 2000.

But another revolution is microbytes away. The information superhighway is on its way and the river of high-tech already flows through our land. This is likely to make as much impact as the inventions of Edison and the Wright Brothers. Nothing will ever be the same—including selling.

New waves for cable surfers

At present, we have one foot in the past and one in the future. Most of the information we use is still recorded on paper, film, and tape. This could change dramatically by the year 2000.

New video compression systems offered by AT&T can carry five separate program signals or up to three hundred channels in the electronic space now used by one channel. Tele-Communications Inc. of Denver, Colorado announced its all-digital compression system which will allow more than five hundred channels to be sent into homes. Technology gurus such as Lawrence Ellison of Oracle Systems and Bill Gates of Microsoft have plans for all these channels.

Lawrence Ellison has a vision. He wants to store the world's text, film, and tapes in huge first-of-a-kind multimedia databases. He wants to create what he calls a "global bazaar" where consumers can shop on a worldwide network, even get loans from foreign banks. At present, Oracle has sales-oriented databases with information on products, customers, salespersons, regions, and time periods. The databases can be tapped by several hundred people simultaneously.

Gates is directing a similar project informally described as "information-at-your-fingertips" through software said to "synchronize the flow of data on the network" and make interactive TV "mindlessly simple" for consumers.

Interactive TV

With deregulation and the coming merger of cable TV and phone companies, we will probably have only one wire into our homes in the near future, leading to a hybrid computer-phone-TV-fax-printer. New technology now being developed by such firms as Microsoft and Oracle Systems will enable subscribers to choose from hundreds of channels and interact with them in a way never before possible.

Want to see *Home Alone XII*? Punch it up on the remote. Not only will viewers be able to call up movies at any time, without regard to program schedules, they will be able to choose camera angles and plot variations. Want to buy a fridge? Order it from a shopping channel, maybe one specializing in household appliances. Consumers will be able to shop till they drop—off to sleep, that is—in their recliners.

Feel like playing the latest video game? Push the right buttons and you are on that network. Forgot to call someone at the office? Turn on the video-conferencing function and talk to them "in person." Want a printed copy of the information on your screen? Just press "print." Need a date? Call up the Virtual Reality channel. It's cheaper and you don't have to agonize over a wine list.

Peter Sealey, marketing chief of Coca Cola, calls these consumers of the not-too-distant future, "TV viewers on steroids." Some of this—the Virtual Reality channel, for example—is still a fair piece down the road. But shopping networks are already here. So are movie channels. The difference is purely one of sophistication.

The most immediate of these interactive television projects is the Time Warner–US West experiment airing in selected cities in 1994. The channels cover, among other subjects, military affairs, health and fitness, therapy, and golf. Viewers will be able to interact in a variety of ways including accessing more detailed information, responding to question-and-answer sessions, ordering products by remote control, and in other ways. According to ad executive David Verklin, this coverage is only the tip of the iceberg. In fact, he predicts "hundreds of interactive channels reaching 25 percent of American households by 1997." Another prediction, one to warm the cockles of consumers' hearts, is that interactive TV will cost only a few dollars more than current cable.

Over seven thousand computers are already working together in an Internet service called the World Wide Web which reaches seventy-five countries with forty-eight thousand different networks. Another seventy-seven countries can send and receive Internet E-mail. Internet traffic can travel over phone lines, cable TV, satellite, wireless phones, or high-speed fiber-optic trunks. Some 21,700 "storefront addresses" are officially registered on the Internet. Intel, Hewlett-Packard, IBM, and Apple Computer are building CommerceNet, an Internet marketplace for electronic goods and services.

There are over seven hundred electronic malls and specialty stores available for cyberspace shopping. You can even attend an on-line Tupperware party. Internet Shopping Network now owns Home Shopping Network and sells over fifteen thousand computer items. Hello Direct hopes its electronic catalog will replace its mail order service for selling telephone accessories on-line. They like the lower costs and the two-way flow of information between customer and supplier. Customers get more product information and use E-mail for product suggestions and technical support.

"With the Internet, the whole globe is one marketplace," according to Bill Washburn, former executive director of Commercial Internet Exchange. Not only can companies reach new companies, but they will have all kinds of opportunities to save money. By linking buyers and sellers and eliminating paperwork, "the cost per transaction will go through the floor," he predicts. The Net can be used for marketing, sales, and customer support as well as a low-cost alternative to fax, express mail, and to establish ongoing relationships with customers.[1]

"The Internet, which blankets the nation and the world, gives small companies an unprecedented opportunity to expand their reach," says Stephen Solomon in *Inc.* magazine. "An electronic storefront on the Internet—open round-the-clock, seven days a week—costs as little as $1,000 a year."[2]

"The economy of scale is enormous," concurs Kitty Weldon, an analyst with the Yankee Group, a consulting firm in Boston. "Where else could a small company afford to advertise to more than 20 million people?"[3]

Dun & Bradstreet Corp. plans to sell and deliver credit reports over the Net. R.H. Donnelly plans to create a World Wide Web–based sales directory. Viewers will be able to click a button on an ad and view the firm's electronic catalog or place an order.

Through an interactive computer service called the "Home-buyer's Fair," builders in the Washington, D.C. area can reach potential buyers on Internet, and potential buyers can access data on fifteen hundred new home communities. Users select a geographic area, click the mouse, and a complete listing of information including pricing, plan size, and builders appears on the screen.[4]

A joint venture with America Online and Shoppers Express will include several supermarket chains and will offer grocery ordering and delivery in more than 40 percent of the country. Customers can order via computer, fax, or phone and specify a ninety-minute period in which their order is delivered. Shoppers can take advantage of in-store specials and coupons, and payment is made via debit card, check, credit card, and electronic funds transfer, through an ATM card. For cybershoppers the blue-light special could become a blinking cursor special as online grocery shopping goes mainstream.[5]

NBC Marketing offers an Interactive service. Advertisers such as Anheuser-Busch, Braun, Chrysler, General Electric, General Motors, and Sea-Doo offer a specialized on-air "800" information line called NBC Viewer Service. NBC also launched NBC Online with T.G.I. Friday's offering the first network/advertiser online promotion. According to their ad, "These are some of the ways we've expanded our horizons in an effort to expand your market. So turn on the tube, pick up the phone, go to a restaurant, open a magazine, log on a computer and board a plane. Wherever your audience is, NBC Marketing is there . . . and we can take you there."[6]

Interactive Network, Inc. formed Charter Advertiser Consortium to develop and test interactive television advertising and promotion. Chrysler tested the system with ads for the Neon, their new small car, during the 1994 Super Bowl with a wireless laptop device. Chrysler challenged subscribers in Chicago, San Francisco, and Sacramento to predict plays for each upcoming down, matching their predictions with those made by Tampa Bay head coach Sam Wyche. Viewers were then asked to participate in a survey on Neon advertising. Over 95 percent agreed to be quizzed. Over 70 percent correctly identified the settings for all three Neon ads and 78 percent grasped Chrysler's strategy of selling the car at both Dodge and Plymouth dealerships. This makes it clear that although consumers want interactive television for such activities as calling plays or requesting their favorite movies, advertising segments also seem to garner a fair share of a consumer's attention as well.

"In the late 1980s we realized that if we were going to stay in business, we'd have to change the way we do things . . . "

Chrysler spokesman Scott Fosgard says. "When you apply that to marketing, you say, 'Do we want to do what everybody else does, or do we want to explore and be ahead of the game?' We know it's coming, so we've got to address the new technology and see how it fits."[7]

United Airlines plans to become the first U.S. airline to go interactive. "United will be the first U.S. carrier to become interactive in the true sense of the word—all business services, faxes, videogames, theater reservations, shopping," said Bill Kopp, president of GEC-Marconi Inflight Systems in Bellevue, Washington, United's interactive systems provider. "Certainly it makes United more competitive and will drive other carriers to make similar decisions."[8]

Warner Bros. will soon offer an electronic version of their retail stores and have contracted with Pacific Data Images in Sunnyvale, California to make TV shopping entertaining, not just convenient. Bugs Bunny and the Tasmanian Devil will guide you through their cyberstore and show you their products.

Most interactive marketing won't be so entertaining, according to Paula George Tompkins, chief executive officer of The SoftAd Group, a Mill Valley, California creator of interactive marketing materials. Instead, they are full of information which will help buyers make complex decisions such as choosing a car or an industrial-products supplier. Their clients include Abbott Labs, Ford, and PPG Industries.[9]

Media specialists tell us the typical American now spends 9 percent of his or her nonworking, nonsleeping time gathering information about products. The greatest amount of this time is the approximately 18 percent of network and cable TV time devoted to advertising. Americans spend more than 30.6 billion hours watching TV ads every year. A majority of these ads are considered a nuisance.[10]

Will consumers be standing in line to get on-line? According to a 1993 CBS News/*New York Times* poll, more than half of adults say they are not interested in interactive television for banking or shopping, but are primarily interested in seeing their favorite TV shows whenever they want. Seventy-seven percent of adults would be happy to sign up.[11] Once viewers sign up for movies they will start experimenting with banking and shopping services.

On-line ordering has become successful in France with 5 million French households having access to a twenty-four-hour electronic marketplace via the Minitel online system. Part of its success can be attributed to the fact that the government distributed free computer terminals that connect to household phones.

According to Robert M. Shapiro, senior vice president for commercial marketing at Prodigy Services, the big advertisers are financial services, auto makers, and computer hardware and software companies.

For more information on electronic malls contact CyberShoppe at 619 794-9522; Branch Mall at 313 741-4442; and Global Network Navigator at 800 998-9938.

Advertising, marketing and selling will merge

Media technology has erased the lines between advertising, marketing, and selling as more ways become available for consumers to shop interactively by phone, TV, or computer. As video-on-demand becomes more commonplace, the media choices available to advertisers will become more fragmented. Traditional advertising will continue to lose audience and market share. Any way you look at it, tomorrow's world will do much of its selling and buying electronically. Consumers will punch up a new suit from Hong Kong and brie from France. Shopping will be a global affair. Understanding and finding new ways to sell through the new media will place innovative companies and salespeople miles ahead of their competitors on the information highway.

"Advertising will become as database-driven as retailing," says Bruce MacEvoy, senior research psychologist at SRI International. "It will shift from selling the product, whatever it may be, to informing only those who really want to know. That is because the real economic and personal value of information often derives from its scarcity, novelty, and relevance to the individual."[12] He believes the feeling and tone of advertising will change from a distant, status-driven appeal to an intimate relationship, more of a playful adventure. In many cases, advertising and entertainment

will merge to become "infotainment," but will be more entertain
ing than our present-day infomercials.

Some of the advertising agencies that specialize in on-line
advertising include Internet Distribution Services in Palo Alto,
California; Open Market in Cambridge, Massachusetts; and
O'Reilly & Associates in Sebastopol, California; as well as the
Online Ad Agency and Messner, Vetere, Berger, McNamee,
Schmetterer, Auro RSCG in New York.

Infomercials

During the '80s we began to see the potential of TV "infomercials," thirty- to sixty-minute commercials dressed up as regular
programs. After a shaky start, infomercials have gained respectabil-
ity and are now recognized as legitimate sales tools. Companies that
once viewed them with a jaundiced eye—Chrysler, Saturn, and
Clairol, to name a few—have climbed on the bandwagon. In the
future we will see infomercials utilized by a greater number of
major companies and upgraded with higher entertainment value.
Commercials will be directed toward specific markets and will
appear on demographically targeted programs and channels.

Most infomercials are direct sales vehicles with "800"
numbers. But, they can be risky business. Only one in ten work
(one in six with a celebrity). Although less expensive than
network advertising, a thirty- to sixty-minute infomercial still
costs from $100,000 to $900,000 to produce. Success, when it
comes, can be sudden and startling. For example, Trillian Health
Products of Seattle boosted its revenues from $6.6 million to
$100 million in two years, using infomercials. A program about
wills hosted by actor John Ritter sold more than a million audio
and videotapes, priced up to $90 each.

The effectiveness of infomercials can be gauged almost
immediately, while results of conventional ads may take months
to compile. This is why, according to Katie Williams, traditional
ad agencies try to discredit them. Williams, who is the world's
biggest producer and time-buyer of infomercials, says traditional
ads are "into creating an image and feeling more than selling."[13]

Direct sales

Perhaps the most dynamic media phenomenon is direct sales, where the use of databases brimming with prospect profiles has increased effectiveness through the mails and on television.

Although the concept has been around for decades, direct advertising on TV has usually been relegated to hours even an owl wouldn't keep. The ads, hokey and frenetic, have been a staple of comedians from Johnny Carson to Robin Williams. Nowadays, the laughs have been replaced by an awed "*hmmmm*." Lately, nobody is kicking sand in the face of direct advertising, which has become a multi-million-dollar hunk.

Already, viewers are ordering merchandise from the Home Shopping Network and QVC, as well as from spot commercials for juicers, compact disks, and home workout centers. It's simple. Just pick up the phone and place an order. In the future, it will be even simpler.

What this means for the selling profession:

- More choices
- More receptive audiences
- Larger audiences
- Immediate profitability
- No middle man
- Unlimited opportunity

How do you get your product on a home shopping network? The odds are about a hundred to one, but don't give up. Contact them to see when their vendor day is and ask for a product-information form. Or you can pay an agent to do it for you for a percentage of sales. Merchandise with a wide appeal that can be demonstrated seems to work best—other than jewelry. Of course, if cash is no problem you can launch your own home-shopping channel. Test market it in your local area at a low cost before you try the big time. In the future expect to see the shopping channels more specialized for niche marketing. Punch up the book channel if you want to check out the new books, or the medical channel if you need a new wheelchair. Basically they will become video catalogs with partnerships between vendors and distributors.

Commercial free TV

Another blow against commercials comes from the world of technology. A 1993 survey by the Roper Organization revealed that 51 percent of adults respond to TV commercials with annoyance. About 47 percent of respondents occasionally change channels when a commercial comes on and about 36 percent occasionally mute the sound.[14]

For around $200 viewers can already screen out commercials by purchasing a Commercial Brake from Arista Technologies. The device hooks to a VCR and automatically eliminates commercials from whatever is being taped. When a program is played back and a commercial starts to come on, the screen fades to blue and the device signals the VCR to fast scan through the commercial, a process which takes about eight seconds, until the program comes back on.

In the future, consumers will limit their commercial viewing to only those messages they want to hear or are paid to hear. Paying selected demographic markets to listen to or watch your commercial will become more popular. For example, selling music on music channels and Harry Hart's FreeFone Information Network (see Chapter 9 on telemarketing).

Plans are afoot to provide viewers with the option of watching programs without commercials for a nominal fee of less than a dollar per program. This service will probably be used mostly by affluent viewers. Still, its presence is likely to have the effect of goading TV advertising into being even more creative.

With so many viewers already giving TV commercials the cold shoulder and with technology making this even easier, more advertisers will shy away from mass market ads and zero in on targeting specific markets.

"Once media becomes interactive and consumers can separate the advertising from the editorial components of media, this system of advertising—financed media—will collapse," says James H. Snider, co-author of *Future Shop*.[15]

This trend has sounded an alarm among traditional mass-market advertisers. Edwin L. Artzt, chairman of Procter & Gamble Co., has warned the American Association of Advertising Agencies that the industry is too slow to react to rapid technological changes in the way information is delivered to consumers. Referring to the era in which viewers will have hundreds of programming choices with no advertising at all, he comments that if advertising is no longer needed to pay most of the cost of home entertainment, then advertisers like P&G (who spend $3 billion per year on advertising) will have a hard time achieving the reach and frequency needed to support their brands. "Television is the lifeblood of our business and we must protect our access to it," said Artzt. "We've got to get together as an industry to better define the video market of the future. This needs to be a collaborative industry effort because we are all in the same boat with our anchors down."[16]

Narrowcasting

Another trend in the new era will be the rise of "narrowcasting," in which channels will be highly specialized and directed toward segmented, rather than mass, audiences. This proliferation of channels and pinpointing of markets should spur competition and reduce advertising costs. A business making walkers, for example, might more effectively advertise on a medical channel, even though the commercial reaches fewer viewers than mass broadcasting. A thirty-second spot might sell for a fraction of what it would cost on network TV.

Demographically selected groups will be the target of much specialized programming. Businesses, airplanes, airports, health clubs, hospitals, medical offices, restaurants, schools, child care centers, and other specific groups will have channels for their special needs. Company-owned and industry-wide television networks are bringing programming to thousands of locations. Business TV is becoming big business. Both McDonald's and Burger King are already test marketing children's videos in their play areas. J.C. Penney, GTE Corporation, and Capital Cities, ABC, Inc. are jointly developing a system for shopping malls.[17]

Customized commercials

Some advertisers want to tailor their commercials for several channels. Coca Cola Classic, for example, runs twenty ads—a variation on a theme—on as many outlets. One for MTV, one for Hispanic TV, one for Chinese TV, and so on. Many experts believe ads in the future will be of shorter duration than they are now, with most lasting less than six months.

Ownership of programs

Remember the old days when some radio and TV shows were brought to you by certain companies like Hallmark, Westinghouse, and GE? U.S. Borox presented Ronald Reagan and *Death Valley Days*. Lipton Tea brought us Arthur Godfrey. Proctor & Gamble CEO Artzt suggests we consider going back to that era. He urged marketers to once again become involved in the development and ownership of prime-time television series, much as they were in the early days of radio and television. "Not all new programming will be available to advertisers," he said, so he recommends that advertisers participate in the ownership of some programming, including sports, video games, and news programs. "We've got to get involved in programming to make certain that advertisers have access to the mass audience and to the best properties," said Artzt, whose company owns three daytime soap operas and some beauty pageant productions.

Customizing the New Media

Newspapers

During the 1960s newspapers were read by 80 percent of the adult population. In 1992 that figure dropped to 68 percent. Television, radio, magazines, and electronic media have taken their toll on newspapers, which has also resulted in an advertising slowdown in the last few years. The recession and changing reader habits have reduced the profitability once enjoyed during the boom years of the mid-eighties.

Technology is bringing new options to newspapers. Using satellite communications, both the *Wall Street Journal* and *USA*

Today are printed simultaneously at multiple sites every day. Some newspapers are now linking up with smart phones and cable TV, where news and classifieds—some with videos—can be pulled up on-screen by viewers. This idea already has been test-marketed on a modest basis with mixed results. The marriage of newspaper and cable expertise will likely tilt the scales. If so, the concept will likely enjoy options similar to other advertising, such as target marketing, narrowcasts, and optimal time slots.

Newspapers across the country are joining together and forming alliances to experiment with alternatives to newsprint and ink, such as computer on-line versions of newspapers. A new group called Partners Affiliated for Exploring Technology (PAFET) invests in research on information technology to collect, package, and market information, making use of the best available evolving technologies.

Phoenix Newspapers has aligned with PressLine, a telephone information service that receives about 8 million calls a year. They offer Home Buying Choices, a real estate information guide accessible by computer modem, telephone, fax, or magazine. They have discovered that new technology will deliver more information to consumers in a variety of forms without the space limitations of print, where much of the information is thrown away or stored.

Classifacts of Denver, Colorado, links buyers and sellers by telephone in local and remote locations. All calls for classified advertising are funneled through a central office by an "800" number which participating newspapers use. Operators create computerized lists of all classified ads in the requested subject area for both the caller's geographical area and all across the nation. Obviously they wouldn't be requesting garage sale information, but they might use the national ads to find a collector's item or obtain information about an area.

Computer systems will create personalized newspapers by logging onto news-service databases at night, selecting stories and pictures, laying them out, and setting the headlines in sizes that reflect their importance to the reader.

In the near future we will see more on-line newspapers allowing readers to interact with the information bases. For example, *The Kansas City Star* offers an audio-electronic link whereby callers can access information, including musical selections related to articles in the paper.

Many newspapers now offer phone-accessible fax delivery of articles and special reports. *USA Today's* popularity seems to be based on consumers who are browsers rather than readers. Short stories, charts, and graphs have attracted a large segment of the population. And if you're aboard ship, don't be surprised when an abridged version of the *New York Times*, TimesFax, is slipped under your cabin door. Oceansat, a satellite news distribution service, makes the publication available to subscribers worldwide. For more information fax TimesFax at 212 727-4802.

Magazines of the future

Many magazines are experimenting with a format other than print. Some magazines are on CD-ROM, allowing the reader to interact, play with, order from, and manipulate the information on a PC. On-line magazine junkies can use personal computers to keep up with their favorite publications. So many magazines are available on-line it is hard to obtain a realistic estimate because new ones are added daily.

The *Newsweek InterActive, National Geographic, Consumer Reports, Kiplinger's,* and *Home Office Computing* are available from Prodigy Services Company. The bottom inch of the screen has advertising copy which users can interact with at any time. America Online offers *Time, Scientific American, Atlantic Monthly, Road & Track,* and *Car & Driver.* Computer movies and animations relating to stories make this more exciting than print. *U.S. News and World Report* on CompuServe includes searchable back issues and College Fair, which ranks individual schools. IBM's electronic equivalent to *Think* magazine (on Internet's World Wide Web) promotes the company, its products, and services.

"Accessing magazines on-line offers full interactive involvement. Text is not the most important part of what happens on-line; it's the communication afterwards," says Jonathan Bulkeley, general manager of media for America Online in Vienna, Virginia. "People talk to each other. They can access any part of the on-line version [of the publication] to back up what they're talking about or to do research on a topic that interests them."[18]

Bulkeley believes the interactive factor makes up for the lack of eye-catching advertising in online magazines. Every time a subscriber accesses a particular publication America Online pays royalties to publishers. "Think of each magazine as having its own room," explains Bulkeley. "Any time anyone opens the door and goes into the room, the magazine makes money."

Radio

Radio, the grandpa of mass media, just keeps on going, and going, and going . . . As times change, it reinvents itself. When television usurped it as the dominant medium, it switched to a music format with great success. Now, with the public more politically aware, it has moved into talk radio big-time—again, with great success. Radio is the most personal of all media, and it can be listened to while working, driving, or playing. It is an effective selling tool and is significantly less expensive than television. Appearances by authors equipped with "800" numbers, for example, have generated volume sales of books that would be impossible through the meager budgets of publishing houses. In fact, some books never see the inside of a bookstore.

Direct-response radio marketing is still in its infancy but is generating lots of interest due to its cost-effectiveness, especially when used as part of a dual-media campaign. With the proliferation of cellular phones, direct-response radio advertising may represent the greatest growth opportunity.

Gary Fries, president-CEO of Radio Advertising Bureau, believes the cellular phone can be a valuable tool for radio advertisers and deserves its own lane on the information superhighway as a direct-response tool. According to the Cellular Telecommunications Industry Association, seventeen thousand Americans sign up for new cellular service each day. As of June 30, 1994, the U.S. cellular phone industry serviced 19 million people, a 3.3 million subscribership increase from January of 1994.[19]

When listeners respond to a phone number on a national broadcast and give their name, address, and phone number to an operator, software such as that developed by Edison Direct of New York will automatically fax the leads to local offices.

Customized pay radio, broadcast over the speaker on your hands-free car phone, seems to be just over the horizon. PacTel and Gannett are launching a joint venture in California that will offer a few minutes of "customerized" news and information to cellular phone subscribers. Each subscriber's broadcast will include news on topics the individual subscriber has requested in advance.[20]

Catalog sales

It's been said that QVC (the world's largest shopping network) is what the Sears catalog should have become. The Sears catalog, as we know, was more than a way to order merchandise. It was more than tradition. It was part of American folklore. But it went the way of buggy whips and rumble seats because it no longer served a purpose. It no longer sold enough to justify its existence. People change; society changes; technology changes—the Sears catalog did not. And it was history for a while, but it's coming back with a series of specialty catalogs. In the future more catalogs will be on-line and available through CD-ROM, as many already are. Read Chapter 6 on CD-ROMs for more information.

Rodney Joffe, president of American Computer Group Inc., says that traditionally it costs between $10 and $15 to process a phone or mail order. On the Internet that cost falls to $4.[21]

Robert Redford's Sundance Catalog sells American handicrafts through its electronic catalog on the Web. When a consumer clicks the "buy" button on a particular item, the computer checks inventory to make sure it's in stock and will try to cross-sell a related item.

Lillian Vernon has become successful with her print catalog but is planning on an electronic future. "We've started . . . We're talking to other people about [home shopping TV] programs. And I think we'll just go into it; I don't have to leap into it . . . but I feel that these are very viable future opportunities for us—additional opportunities to what we have now."[22]

Chrysler Corp. included a CD-ROM new car buyers' guide with *Multimedia World* in January of 1995, adding video and sound to the usual product catalog. It's also available to prospects who call an "800" number seeking product information. Users will be able to access product specifications and options information, view the model inside and out from different angles, and even change the vehicle's color.

Some of the best catalogs around offer a cooperative program with ScanFone. Just pick up the penlight on your ScanFone, scan the bar code representing Hammacher Schlemmer, Barnes & Noble, or other catalog of your choice, scan the item number, run your credit card through your phone slot, and the item will be shipped to you without ever talking to a real live person. Not only that, but you get discounts from participating catalogs for using your ScanFone.

Of course, not everything will change overnight. Paper is still more economical for many people than a computer. Others feel more comfortable turning the pages of a book than pulling up text on a monitor. There are also selling approaches that, because of their indirect nature, are unlikely to change.

Catalogs on diskettes

Diskalog, Inc. will conduct a free cost-savings audit for companies considering replacing their paper-based catalogs with catalogs on diskettes. Contact them at 312 853-4774.

MiniCat, from Prostar Interactive MediaWorks, sells software for $199 that lets users combine text and scanned images to make floppy-disk catalogs. Call 604 273-4099.

Cable cops

The new media offer unlimited opportunities for direct marketing and sales. But make sure you stay within the best interests of the consumers, helping them find what they want rather than tricking them. In some cases, companies should even enhance their competitors' opportunities and interests, like the Santa in the movie *Miracle on 34th Street*. If Macy's didn't have what the customers wanted, rather than try to convince them to change their minds, he told them where they could find the item, even if it was from a competitor.

Any hint that consumers are being exploited or controlled will greatly hinder future marketing success. For example, *Newsweek* reported an incident involving a title fight that was carried over pay cable. A commercial was aired offering a free T-shirt to those who responded. It was set up, however, so only those who were illegally tapped into the fight saw the commercial. When people responded to the ad, they received a form letter informing them of their illegal cable tapping and offering to settle for $2,000.

Mass media vs. new media

Assembly-line technology made mass production possible, but it was the emergence of mass media that led to the development of mass media marketing, or awareness advertising. In the future, companies will be talking more and more to individual customers, not to large groups with the hope that someone is listening. Electronic media is already cheaper than the U.S. mail.

According to Bruce MacEvoy, senior research psychologist at SRI International in Menlo Park, California, change leaders will be the first to change channels; the best ways to reach them are through the emerging media such as computers, interactive TV, and customized publications. The new media's messages will be more intimate, playful, and individualistic.

The most important thing to grasp about new media, says MacEvoy, is that cultural expectations are now overtaking technological capabilities. New media are more than new communication resources; they define a way of life. The new media may become mainstream media or they may not. Either way, new media will reinforce the social networking activities of change leaders. They will also boost consumer expectations for variety, novelty, personalization, interactivity, and freedom from unwanted information. Ultimately, they could even encourage age, ethnic, and other kinds of segregation in American society.[23]

How do you get there from here?

Thompson Publishing Group offers subscribers a valuable resource guide, *Electronic Marketplace Sourcebook*, which covers online services and the Internet, infomercials and home shopping, interactive kiosks, telephones and television, CD-ROMS, video conferencing, and legal issues. Included are listings of vendors, service bureaus, advertising and production agencies, associations, publications and attorneys who specialize in the new media. Available for $349 a year. Call 800 879-3169.

Part II

Sales Automation—
Result-Enabling Technologies
(Computers and Phones)

Chapter 4

A Bit of This, a Byte of That
(Computers)

*"What's happening in the end of the 20th century is the ability
to use computers is the functional equivalent to reading, writing,
and arithmetic."*

—Mark Cooper
Consumer Federation of America

Al Cohn, marketing manager for commercial systems engineering at Goodyear Tire & Rubber, helps five hundred salespeople and field engineers utilize six years' worth of performance
data stored on Goodyear's mainframes. The databank includes
statistics on tread wear, durability, and fuel economy, as well as
information on pricing, tire sizes, and competitors' products.
During a sales call the salespeople hook into the mainframe by
phone and can get answers to specific customer questions. For
example, if a customer asks, "How does this tire perform on a
Mack truck that hauls coal in Kentucky with an average load of
6,000 pounds per tire?" in ten seconds a graph is generated on
the on-site computer and can be printed out for the customer on
the spot.

According to Cohn, in the pre-computer days people would
ask questions like this and we'd say, "Sure, let us look in our
files, and we'll get back to you in two weeks." Cohn recommends this mainframe/PC system for selling any industrial

product that has extensive data associated with it, from chemicals to corporate jets.[1]

Salespeople in the twenty-first century will depend heavily upon modern technology for their competitive edge. When properly applied, technology creates value. Increasing the value of services through computer systems will help salespeople operate more efficiently and improve the bottom line.

In 1985 Metropolitan Life Insurance Company equipped its agents with hand-held computers so they could tally policy premiums. In 1988 they upgraded to Honeywell 286 laptops for their needs-selling presentations. Recently they traded up to the 386. During this time MetLife's sales have set records. They now have more insurance in force than any other company and have led the industry in sales for the last three years. Their sales force dropped from twenty-five thousand to thirteen thousand in fifteen years. According to Dean Holmes, senior supervising consultant for personal insurance financial management at MetLife's New York headquarters, computers have enabled account reps to service clients better by equipping them to:

- Run through their needs-selling presentations with prospects in a professional and efficient manner
- Instantly access information about customers, and keep files up-to-date
- Quickly calculate rates for a wide variety of the company's products[2]

It's quite simple: lack of information can lead to lost sales. Data equals knowledge and knowledge is power. Real-time information is often the difference between a closed door and a closed sale. Salespeople who are able to give their customers the most information in the shortest amount of time win.

Why should salespeople use computers?

Each year *Sales & Marketing Management* magazine conducts a survey of PC usage and sales. Their most recent survey (a sampling of over five thousand) revealed four out of five respondents experienced higher sales productivity from computer usage. The average gain for 1992 was 20 percent. The number one reason for the rise in sales was increased efficiency in following up clients and clients' leads.

By contrast, a Cahnes Publishing survey of four thousand companies in 1992 revealed that 41 percent of their customers were not contacted by sales reps in the prior year because of lack of good records.

You may be one of those individuals who can remember all your prospects and clients' names, addresses, and interests. Most of us can't. Use your brain for strategy and use a computer to remember the details—clients' spouses and childrens' names, a complete history of their sales records, upcoming needs, the best time to contact them, and a myriad of other information to help improve your productivity.

Time management and greater sales call frequency are also high-priority common reasons for using a computer. Eleven percent of the salespeople used the computer to formulate complete proposals on their laptops while in front of the buyer, trying to shorten the sales cycle by giving the customer the capability for faster buying decisions. Others use computers for developing effective marketing plans.

A computer allows you to publish your sales materials, price sheets, bids, brochures, newsletters, and other literature as though you had a full typesetting, graphics, and print shop. Then it functions as your mailing service.

Salespeople catering to professional contractors, designers, or do-it-yourself customers often deal with hundreds or thousands of items. Computer literate sales people can access product specs, building codes, regulations, and design specs, as well as create computer-assisted designs to plan or design the project.

Complex and time-consuming mathematical calculations on your bids or specifications can be performed on your PC in a matter of minutes or seconds.

Let's consider the area of order processing:

Old way: Take the order by writing it down on a scrap piece of paper or phone pad, transfer it to a typewriter, turn it in to the order desk, then add it to the sales log, inform the shipping department, accounting department, assembly room, etc.

Computer way: Information is entered once with ready access by all departments. In addition, the one-time entry into the computer also enables sales management to retrieve this information if the salesperson is out of the office or leaves the company.

When salespeople make inquiries or send in orders from the field, they can immediately check the status of orders from sales to shipping to accounting. The billing is faster, checks come in sooner, and suppliers are able to be paid during the early payment discount time frame. They can use their fax modem to send out quotes, transmit rush orders to suppliers, mail reminder notices for bills, etc.

Other important reasons to use a computer:

• word processing	• customer correspondence
• account management	• spreadsheets
• client/prospect info	• E-mail
• call reports	• proposal preparation
• sales presentations	• call planning
• sales forecasts	• sales analysis
• graphics	• order entry
• territory management	• direct marketing
• budget preparation	• mapping
• check inventory control	• shipping status
• telemarketing	• market analysis

Every day people find new ways to use technology and access new information. Even if you aren't going to use new technology to create a new product or business as some have done, you can profit from it in many small ways. Some salespeople swap information informally with one another on-line. Besides networking, they share selling ideas and industry information. It is also a great tool for building relationships with customers, and to manage information and accounts with greater efficiency. Let's look at how technology has changed the way real estate is sold.

Selling real estate by computer

Buying a house can be a long, tedious process, but computer technology is making it easier—and more fun—in some cities.

"Before computers, multiple listing books consisted of several books the size of a large telephone directory," says real estate agent Dean Selvey. "Today, most realtors use the computerized version of MLS, which is updated on a daily basis. A data base of tax records also allows realtors to access information immediately about a specific home."[3]

If you're thinking of moving to the Sun Belt, Homes by Computer is a free electronic service offered by the *Arizona Republic* and the *Phoenix Gazette*. The service, which gives you details about homes that meet your needs, is available any time to anyone with a computer and modem. Homes found within this service also are advertised in the *Republic* and *Gazette*, *Home Buying Choices* magazine, and Home Choices By Phone. Home Choices By Computer offers a mortgage calculator, interest rate updates, a directory of realtors and real estate news and information. To access the Homes By Computer services, set your software to 8N1 and dial 440-HOME (4663).

SMILE in New York City and HomeView in Needham, Massachusetts will help you buy a new home. If you don't feel like fighting traffic and spending days in the car touring properties, go to one of their offices, use their interactive full-color databases, and have a visual tour of the properties of your choice. If you shop at SMILE there is no charge. If you sell through Smile you pay $75 per month for a listing. If you're a broker you pay $1,000 up front and $500 per year to subscribe. HomeView doesn't charge until the sale is complete, then the brokers pay a commission. SMILE operates worldwide and specializes in high-end properties.[4]

HomeView Realty Centers computers in Boston contain color pictures of every house listed by brokers in Massachusetts—about twenty-two thousand at any one time. Buyers can sit down at a computer terminal and scan towns in Massachusetts, looking at the streets, the shopping centers, the library, the town hall, and the schools. With the flick of a button they can access demo graphic information on the town, its school system, taxes, commuting times, and other points of interest.

After prospective buyers choose a town, they start a house search by listing their price range and the type and size of lot and house they want. Then they add options like fireplace, number of bedrooms, air-conditioning, and rank them by "must have" or "would like to have." When all the requirements are put in, a menu screen appears with photos of the houses that fit those descriptions. Touch the one you want and the screen displays a picture of that house. Touch it again and up comes a menu of which areas of the house you want to tour. Want to see the yard and surrounding area? Touch that option and it's on the screen.

HomeView says its customers visit six houses, on average, compared with twenty for typical home buyers, and most find a house they want to buy in less than thirty days. There's no extra charge for the HomeView service. HomeView agents split the real estate commission with listing brokers, just as other agents do who bring in a home buyer.[5]

In Minnesota, Burnet Realty and Edina Realty, which rank in the top ten of real estate companies nationally by the number of sales and sales volume, have each spent from $1 million to $5 million developing different computer systems.

Burnet's system links its thirty-eight realty sales offices to the forty-eight First Security Title and Great Lakes Mortgage offices, enabling Burnet managers and salespeople to give home buyers and sellers up-to-the-minute information about their home-sale file. They have instant access to credit reports, appraisals, employment verification, title orders, mortgage, insurance, tax data, mapping, schools, and other information.

Edina's system links its fifty-nine sales offices and the forty-six Equity Title and Metropolitan Federal Bank mortgage offices. Their database management program enables managers to know how well their offices are doing in terms of sales and budgeting at any given time.

Both companies' systems have a database of their own listings which includes full motion, interactive videos of the exterior and interior of listings, a map with information about nearby schools, churches, and other landmarks, property tax breakdowns, and demographic data about the neighborhood—average home price, average family and lot sizes. They will also include their competitors' listings through the Regional Multiple Listing Service. All of this information will be accessible to each of their agents via laptop computers.

Scott Schmaren of Arlington Heights, Illinois runs classified ads in CompuServe which gives him worldwide exposure to potential customers moving to the Chicago area. He also uses the service's messaging capabilities to find leads for local clients who are relocating elsewhere. "Using a computer is not going to make you a lot of money directly," Schmaren says, "but it is going to enhance what you already know."[6]

Virtual reality homes? At the Las Vegas convention of the National Association of Home Builders, a prototype of a virtual reality home buying system was demonstrated. Using CAD (computer-aided design) technology, the system will artificially create model homes and customize them to the buyer's tastes. Instead of trying to visualize what it will look like, buyers will be able to see all aspects of their home on the computer before it is built. When available, this system could drastically cut down the cost of building and maintaining so many model homes and help sell new homes.

Are computers worth the money?

Sales and Marketing Management's seventh annual "Survey of PC Usage and Sales" reports that almost two-thirds of the survey respondents say they recouped their investment in sales force automation in only eight months. Firms with less than ten sales reps had the fastest payback and firms with more than one hundred sales reps had the slowest payback. Twenty-three percent say they don't see the need to develop quantifiable measurements. Some use PCs to keep up with competitors and others use them to give salespeople a more professional look. MIT's Sloan School of Management's survey on 400 of the Fortune 500 companies found an average 54 percent return-on-investment on computer purchases.[7]

Inc. magazine conducted a FaxPoll(TM) as a follow-up to their "Guide to Office Technology" issue. Most readers reported that they depend on their computers, faxes, and other high-tech office equipment. Seventy-three percent asserted that their investments in new office technologies have "absolutely" paid for themselves in increased productivity, while another 21 percent acknowledged at least some productivity payoff.[8]

A recent study at one medium-size firm estimated it could save more than $100,000 per year in long-distance telephone costs if even 25 percent of its staff were hooked up to their Internet on-line computer service.

Sales force automation (SFA) now is an important part of research and development for several companies in the computer and information technology business, and it has been identified as a major source of future revenue. IBM has created Sales Force–Integrated Services for project consulting, system integration, hardware, software, and application development, and network connectivity, maintenance, and support. A few of the other companies involved in SFA research are Digital Equipment Corp., Hewlett-Packard, and Apple Computer.

Sales Leadership Strategies, the research and advisory function of Gartner Group, is developing architecture and software applications for sales and marketing systems with special emphasis on the mobile computing communication requirements for field sales reps.

Whatever you call it—sales force automation, computerized marketing, database marketing, or sales support systems—using computers in sales is a proactive, stay-ahead strategy. Bob Ashley, vice president of Realty USA says, "With the market of available buyers shrinking, and more demands on our agents' time, we looked to Sales Automation to dramatically improve agents' personal productivity, overall sales efficiencies and to help improve our builder retention."[9]

The Stone Institute reported that among the home builders and realtors they surveyed who were using computers:

- Closing ratios are up
- Many needless reports and activities are eliminated
- One-on-one sales time with qualified buyers increases
- Costly mistakes are reduced
- Builders love the new reports

- More homes are sold
- More commissions are earned!

In the near future, proficiency with a computer will be almost mandatory in many sales positions. *Selling* magazine reports that 95 percent of their readers who responded to their survey use computers at work. The most common combination for salespeople was both a desktop and a laptop with a built-in fax modem. A PC can do the work of a staff of hundreds or thousands of people. It's like having your own private workforce at your fingertips, enabling you to run your sales territory like your own business. The question is no longer whether to buy but rather which, how powerful, how many, and where to buy.

What kind of software is available?

Deciding which software to buy and spend time learning can be as overwhelming as deciding which computer equipment to purchase. Ask other salespeople which software they use and check it out. Make a list of what you want to do with your computer and ask the computer experts in your company what they recommend. For some of us this is difficult because we can't imagine all the ways we can use the computer without knowing its capabilities.

Salespeople can choose from more than three hundred software packages to manage their client and prospect databases, prepare quotes, handle order entry and billing, and replace daily calendars and "to do" lists.

It's a good idea to decide on your software and hardware before you purchase anything. Take time to read *PCs for Dummies* published by IDG. Contact What to Buy for Business Inc. at 800 829-9097 and order copies of their buying guides for the products you are interested in.

IBM offers a service called "IBM PC Direct" to help create a custom combination of hardware and software tailored to your business and budget. For more information call 800 IBM-2968.

You might also want to contact SoftSearch, a service of Synergy Computer Consulting, in Vancouver, British Columbia. For $125, SoftSearch will prepare a customized report compiling all available references pertaining to a given software title, including articles, reviews, and a demo copy if possible. In addition, they will tap into their extensive software and find commercial programs to fit your particular needs. Call 800 667-6503 for more information.

New Horizons Development Group in Kennett Square, Pennsylvania has developed a field sales software program called MVP that helps salespeople plan and forecast sales, monitor performance, and track profitability by specific account. According to President K. Bruce Koepcke, "MVP addresses the management side of sales force automation because not only does it help salespeople become more efficient at what they already do, but also assists them in running their sales territories as if they were their own businesses."

PDC Generator helps you write reports, marketing plans, and proposals. After asking you questions about the benefits of your products, the software selects the correct document, fills in the blanks, inserts the right phrases, and calculates the equations for you.

Harvey Mackay, author of *Swim with the Sharks*, emphasizes the importance of regular contact with clients and prospects. In conjunction with CogniTech Corporation, Mackay created Sharkware, a user-friendly software which makes it easy to reference and cross-reference the equivalent of several Rolodex files under categories of your choice. It functions as a time management system with a "to do" list, a daily, weekly, and monthly calendar, and an alarm clock. By listing the phone calls you need to make it will not only remind you to call them, but automatically dial them for you.

Top Producer has an automatic letter scheduler. Each day when you turn on your computer it will tell you to print out specific letters for your prospects. Calendar Creator Plus by Power Up! offers a simple-to-use calendar.

An interactive software program named "Howard and Friends" is designed especially for real estate sales and contains a marketing plan, prospect base, calendar, daily planner, and a variety of letters and postcards. PREP is a software program for realtors which creates residential marketing proposals. Pursuit by Information Management Consultants helps prepare quotations.

ACT! by Symantec Corporation is a highly recommended contact manager program for short selling cycles, as well as Telemagic by Mototech Systems. Longer selling cycle products which require dozens of people and several years need different software. Goldmine by ELAN software, WinSales by Winsight Inc., or Maximizer by Sales Implementation Systems not only help you keep track of dozens of contacts, but includes report-writing capabilities so you can communicate with other members of your sales or management team.

ResponsAbility by Concinnate Geneer is a letter-generator that enables you to send out hundreds of customized response letters. Sales LetterWorks by Round Lake Publishing offers three hundred sales letters for prospecting, making appointments, proposals, quotations, thank-you letters, overcoming objections, etc.

Expense It! by On the Go Software helps you track and report your travel expenses. Its built-in expense forms will print directly on your company's forms. It also links up with a Sharp Wizard. Sales managers will find Salescom by Schroeder Associates useful. It helps set up sales compensation plans. Special software for network marketing is available from 20/21 Software, Inc. Call 801 225-8700.

Want to run your own electronic superhighway for just $259? Galacticomm gives you that opportunity and allows you to run your own electronic Bulletin Board Service (BBS) accessible to your clients and associates via modems, LANs, and X.25 networks. The Major BBS is a full-featured multiuser software package for DOS or Windows. With it, you can offer electronic mail, file upload/download, private message forums, and teleconferencing to up to 256 simultaneous users, all from a single PC. Faxmail, Internet connectivity, graphics, multiuser databases, and much more are available as plug-in options. For a free information kit, call 800 328-1128 or fax 305 583-7846.

As always, one of your best resources is to check with experts in your area of sales to find out about software that meets the specific needs of your industry. And if you're still confused, contact Richard Bohn and ask for his newsletter and Sales Automation Survival Guide. Fax him at The Denali Group, 206 391-7982.

What if you don't like computers?

"Some people view a computer as a distasteful typewriter on steroids; they would go back to their typewriter if they could."
—Susan Mitchell

According to a survey by Dell Computer Corp., 55 percent of the population harbors some fear or hesitation about technology, whether it's a personal computer or a VCR. Michelle Weil, a clinical psychologist from Orange, California, says up to one-third of those with technophobia actually experience physical reactions like sweating, nausea, and dizziness.[10]

When Dick Becker started selling insurance for Allstate forty years ago, right out of college, the office didn't even have an electric typewriter. But the days of carbon copies are long gone. Today all the offices are linked to the company's mainframe, and the changes to the policy are made from each sales office. When a client applies for a car insurance policy, Dick uses the computer to pull up the client's driving record from the Department of Motor Vehicles, contact the previous company about an existing or past policy, and check his or her credit rating. If a person comes to Arizona from the East and wants to make changes on the Allstate policy he or she has in another state, Dick pulls up all the policy info on the computer.

Not all the Allstate agents have been anxious to learn how to use the computer, and sometimes the secretaries enter the data for the techno-laggards. Recently at a sales kickoff meeting, Bill Monie, Allstate's vice president for the Rocky Mountain states announced, "If you don't learn how to operate the Allstar system [IBM AS 400] you will be out of business in a couple of years. You can't tell the client, 'I'll have the secretary figure that quote for you.'"

A survey by *Inc.* magazine on office technology revealed that 47 percent of the readers who responded to the survey have a love relationship with their computer. While 24 percent wished they knew how to use it better, 20 percent felt they were its master. Four percent said they're still strangers, 3 percent felt it's just a tool they have to use, and 2 percent found endless frustration with it. Among those who use the computer, many of them use it in several locations—98 percent use it at the office, 76 percent at home, 23 percent on the road, 14 percent calling on customers, and 12 percent on vacation. One-fifth of survey respondents felt that by using the most advanced technology they maintain an edge over competitors.[11]

Salespeople are generally known for their people skills. Many reject technology not only because they dislike it, but they're afraid they'll have to give up personal contact with their clients. However, like Arthur Miller's Willy Loman, we know charm is not enough. Information and service are vital in sales. Simply put, technology makes them more accessible for us.

People in their twenties and thirties grew up with computers and generally are more comfortable with them than people over forty, who frequently view them as a threat. A professor of marketing at San Diego State University, Thomas Wotruba, points out, "There is a generation of salespeople emerging who are not only computer-literate but who also have been weaned on information, customer orientation, TQM, etc."

If you are one of those super salespeople who have made your living for years in sales on a one-to-one basis and have never touched a computer and don't intend to, we're not going to judge you. That's your right. Had you lived ninety years ago you probably would also have stated that no one would catch you in one of those new-fangled Model Ts that crazy Henry Ford dreamed up. A horse and buggy was good enough for your parents and it was good enough for you. You're not alone in this thinking. In 1913 the American Road Congress published the following statement, "It is an idle dream to imagine that . . . automobiles will take the place of railways in the long distance movement of . . . passengers."[12]

"Automation technology is essential in sales," says Gil Cargill, sales productivity consultant in Carson City, California. "Without it, salespeople aren't able to make informed and accurate decisions confidently and instantaneously. In short, they're powerless."

There will always be a need for personal contact with your prospects and clients, and you will possibly be able to scrape by without a computer or any of the technology we mention in this book. You may be hindering your own progress, however. There is a faster, more efficient way. We're not suggesting you go out and buy all the equipment we talk about. You may feel overwhelmed. But then again, it could be empowering. Look at it as a challenge. Learn one new skill until it's comfortable before you try another one. Take it on as a hobby, a learning goal, or a family activity. We also recommend trying one or more of these options:

1. Talk to salespeople you know in your industry who use computer technology. Find out what they have in hardware and software and how it helps them in their selling career.

2. Educate yourself. Read trade and technical magazines for your industry. Start looking for articles that talk about high-tech applications. Make a note of the kind of equipment and software. Read *DOS for Dummies* and *WordPerfect for Dummies* both by Dan Gookin.

3. Contact your local community college and ask them about noncredit classes that introduce computer technology. Initially you might not even know what you want to take, but see if they offer any of the classes you read and heard about in the first two options above. Some community colleges offer a three-hour or one-day class introducing you to the basics. Learn the beginning concepts, then come back and take intermediate and advanced one-day classes. You will be surprised at how much you can learn in one day. Don't worry, the class won't be filled with college kids. They already know the basics. You will find colleagues your age and older who realize progress is going to pass them by if they don't start hitching a ride on the information highway.

4. Buy a computer system that includes a tutorial videotape or buy the tape separately. Call PC Video at 201 478-3606 to inquire about their tutorial series available for about $295.

5. Teach yourself with the tutorial program in the computer and the manuals. The Simplified Accelerated Intelligence Learning System (SAILS) was developed by the research division of CompuClub. SAILS offers a book titled *How to Learn to Operate and Even Program a Computer in One Day with SAILS* for $14.95. For $7.95 you can buy a book

entitled *The 45-Minute Guide to Buying Your First Computer or Upgrading Your Old Computer.* Also available is a computer operation assistance software called PAT (Personal Assistant and Tutor) which provides accelerated learning for all ages. Call 800 586-4629.

6. Ask your kids to show you how to use their computer. Even though they haven't been able to master the art of cleaning their rooms, you'd be amazed at how much they know about computers.

7. Find a friend or an associate who'll gently tutor you through the acquisition and learning process. Look for someone who is sympathetic to your assumed mental block about technology. A codependent person is best for this task.

8. Attend one of the private computer training schools.

9. Take an on-line computer class in the privacy of your home or office, or hire a private tutor.

10. Sign up for a computer seminar. Data-Tech Institute offers six hundred courses nationwide covering data communications and networking, telecommunications, microcomputers, Macintosh, and special interest courses. Call 201 478-5400 for their latest catalog. Seminars can be very helpful for general knowledge, but not always the best learning method if you are trying to learn specific software. Unless you excel in learning by watching, it is very difficult to sit in a hotel room with three hundred people and an instructor a football field away explaining the software's functions. Try all the other options before you subject yourself to this method of learning. It's much easier to learn in a classroom situation where there is one computer per student rather than watching the instructor use a computer on a projection screen—you'll forget everything by the time you get home.

Still don't want to use a computer?

Becoming computer literate is a survival step for the future of your selling career. According to Kerry Fehr-Snyder, computers are great equalizers, bringing one of the most powerful informa tion and communications tools of this century to the average person.[13]

We are living in an information-based society. The successful salesperson will become increasingly dependent on effective and creative use of information technology. Sure, you can continue to sell as you always have, but your competitors are going to be miles ahead of you on the information highway. Without your own computer and a working knowledge of it, you will be forced to hitchhike, or be stranded indefinitely at a rest stop.

Chapter 5

Fishing Where the Fish Are
(High-Tech Prospecting)

"As computing power has made possible more and more detailed analysis, mass marketing has evolved into niche marketing, with companies fighting to define and conquer smaller and smaller segments of consumers."
— Martha Rogers, Ph.D.[1]

Gordie Allen trains salespeople in the art of "power prospecting": how to use computers, faxes, and telephones to book prequalified appointments. He carefully targets his prospects, then, to get their attention, he gives them a sample of his techniques.

Although many office buildings post "no soliciting" signs, thanks to today's technology Allen can get into offices without physically banging on doors. After calling select businesses in a given office area or office building and asking for their fax numbers, he pulls his Jeep into the parking garage, plugs his IBM notebook PC into his car's cigarette lighter and his Motorola cellular phone into the computer, and starts faxing letters to the training department of each business. After a few minutes he calls to make sure they received the material, says he's in the area and asks if he can come by and introduce himself. Some people find his techniques so unbelievable they come down to the garage to check out his setup.

"I'm not a tech junkie," he says, "I just use technology as a tool."[2]

Allen's techniques are just an example of how salespeople use technology to target their market. Old-fashioned prospecting has worked for salespeople for years. Technology has enhanced our ability to identify the best prospects and more easily access a tremendous amount of information and prospective customers, so our efforts will be more productive.

Computer mapping

Desktop geographic information systems (GIS) combine target marketing and numerous databases and display them in map form.

According to Terry Moloney of Tydac Technologies Corporation in Ottawa, Canada:

> You can integrate all the various geographic entity types—such as store locations, the locations of customers' households, zip codes, and census tracts—with line information, such as 'x' number of cars travel this segment of road at 4 P.M. Once integrated, then you can analyze: Who are customers within a mile of my branch with an income over $50,000 who are next to a major thoroughfare?

Atlas Software by Stategic Mapping analyzes market potential by sales territory, distribution coverage by product, or customer locations by zip code or street address. Ask for a free Desktop Mapping Guidebook and demo disk. Phone 408 985-7400, 800 472-6277 or fax 408 985-0859.

Strategic Mapping helped a Minnesota milling company show where livestock are raised in the Midwest, identifying markets for its feed products. "With the increasing horsepower of PC-based systems, you can do more for less," says John Krizek of Strategic Mapping in San Jose.

Before desktop GIS, "you could do it two ways," says Steve Poizner, president of Strategic Mapping, which produces Atlas*GIS. "You could manually draw zip code boundaries on a street map," using pins to show data in a process that could take months.

"The other alternative was using a high-end GIS system," he says. "But they're expensive, they require specialized operators, and they're not tailored to the everyday business guy who's on a deadline and doesn't have a big budget."

Geographic analysis by latitude and longitude makes analysis by zip code seem crude. The zip code offers a mixed clump of people, says Tydac's Moloney, but "a GIS will allow you to get to smaller, more homogeneous geographic levels, even to households."

The Census Bureau offers TIGER (Topologically Integrated Geographic Encoding and Referencing system), which is a digitized street map of the United States. When integrated with GIS products, marketers can produce a map where city blocks with high concentrations of specific households are shaded in red. The GIS can tell you if those concentrations are linked to your target market.[3]

Matchmaker/2000 matches street address ranges to latitude and longitude coordinates so you end up with a useful picture of where your customers and prospects are located. They offer nationwide street coverage, with more than 12 million address ranges, as well as sales effectiveness analyses. They will meet your specific budget and application with a range of expandable and upgradable database options.

Sure! Maps from Horizons Technology Inc. comes on CD-ROM and helps you evaluate sales and marketing information by region and determine market strengths and weaknesses.

Geosight by Sammamish Data Systems Inc. uses your company's data to create maps for target marketing, sales territory management, and market analyses.

Other mapping programs include Scan/US from Scan/US Inc. and GEOvista for Macintosh from Newton Technology. Also check out Geographic Data Technology, Inc. at 800 331-7881.

Find new customers . . . online!

With your PC and a modem, you can tap into a database of 10 million businesses whenever you want, twenty-four hours a day, to retrieve and qualify prospects for your business. You may select by SIC (Standard Industry Classification) code or Yellow

Page–type of category, number of employees, estimated sales volume, contact name, or title for any geographic area. American Business Lists—ONLINE is an instant source of information for sales leads, direct marketing, market research, making credit decisions, and more. Call 402 593-4593 or fax 402 331-6681.

The Major BBS is a tool you can use to reach customers one-to-one. By running your own electronic Bulletin Board System (BBS), your company is available around the clock to everyone with a modem—or through the Internet. Your BBS can serve as a liaison between all the people and information inside your organization and the rest of the world. Every department can have access to the real customer—and vice versa. You can exchange electronic mail with prospects, customers, and the press through the Internet, CompuServe, and other worldwide networks. You can also accept orders online via a catalog shopping facility which can automatically validate credit card orders. Call Galacticomm at 800 328-1128 for more information.

Dun & Bradstreet Information Services brings you information on over 9 million large and small businesses which you can access online with Prodigy. The information you need can be downloaded into mailing labels, full records, and telemarketing records with contact name, location, telephone number, and topic. "If you're a salesperson with a new product idea and you'd like to see who else is in the same area, you could go in by city or state or zip, SIC [Standard Industry Classification], type of location, sales," explains Barbara McCoy, director of D&B's online product development. For more information call D&B at 908 665-5105 or Prodigy at 914 448-2496.

Turn addresses into phone numbers

Are you trying to reach all the homes within a ten-mile radius of your office, or businesses in a certain geographical area? Whatever your needs, if it's a listed number, Telematch will find it for you if you give them the address area. Or, if you have the phone numbers and want the names and addresses, they're easily obtainable. The Phone Number Company in Virginia has over 75 million business and residential phone numbers in their database. For a nominal fee of between two and six cents per listing, they will turn addresses into phone numbers or phone numbers into addresses for you. The minimum charge for phone numbers is $150, and $250 for addresses. If you have an "800" or "900" number, they will provide names and addresses of everyone who calls your number. Their turnaround time can be as little as twenty four hours. For more information call Telematch at 800 523-7346.

Prophone of Marblehead, Massachusetts, has the answer to a salesperson's dream. It took ten thousand phone books and put more than 80 million business and residential phone numbers and addresses on CDs. For $149 you can purchase directPHONE and obtain 72 million nationwide residential listings on a single CD, plus 7.5 million businesses on a separate CD. For $349 you can purchase selectPHONE and search an address for a phone number or a phone number for an address. Or if you prefer, just search by name. All this on four CDs!

Target a specialized niche

Whether you're trying to reach skiers standing in line waiting for the chairlift or convention attendees standing in front of an interactive electronic kiosk, information is available to assist you. Advertising Options Plus (AOP) lists a profile, contact name/number and rate information for over sixteen hundred out-of-home advertising options. With the emphasis on specialization, a variety of companies have compiled the marketing data so you won't have to do your own research.

One more example is a company called Ski Ad which concentrates on snow skiers. Another company, Sitour North America, limits their market to selling ad space in 120 of America's favorite ski resorts.

On the move?

Val-Pak Direct Marketing Systems targets the million families who move each month and sends out Solo Values—postcards and flyer coupons—for more than one thousand clients who want their business. Other demographic segments they reach are new mothers and recent high school graduates. Their database consists of 52 million households and businesses in the United States and

Canada, and are grouped according to type and mail carrier routes into clusters of ten thousand homes called Neighborhood Trading Areas.

Welcome the newcomers

A new family moving into your area will spend more during their first year than the average established household spends in five, according to Solo Values, a national marketing company. These new prospects are open to suggestions on where to take their business. Solo Values offers direct mail programs that specifically identify and target your best new resident prospects using zip codes, recent home purchases, recent movers who reside in single-family dwelling units, new college students, etc.

For example, if you operate a day care center, the Solo Values program can target new families moving into your area with small children. The National Child Care Association suggests that if day care centers offered two weeks of free child care to select people in their target market, they will make an additional $2,240 per year (based on $70/week fee for thirty-two weeks per year) on each customer who takes advantage of this offer.

If you run a fitness center, Solo Values can help you by sending a direct mail offer of thirty days free membership to your target market—college students, for example. According to the International Sports Association, the average annual value of each new customer obtained through this free membership offer is $542 per year. Multiply $542 by the number of new college students in your area each year and watch your sales grow!

Target your market with direct response ads

The ultimate in target marketing is having the customers call you before you identify them. Several technologies are referred to in this book which can be combined to put the prospect right in touch with the seller. These include "800", "900", and "1000" numbers, as well as "reverse 900" numbers, electronic coupons, and fax response systems.

For example, after a long bill-paying session, Diane was sitting in her home in Scottsdale, Arizona, reading *Inc.* magazine, when she saw an ad for Panasonic's Check Printing Accounting

(CPA). Interested in learning more about it, she called the "800" number in the ad expecting voice mail to tell her to punch in her fax number for more information. Instead, she was immediately transferred to Bullock's department store in Scottsdale. Thinking it was a mistake, she dialed again. This time, her call was answered by Office Max in Scottsdale. Realizing it wasn't a mistake, she asked about the CPA, was given the price, and told only one was left in stock so she'd better hurry right over. She did and purchased the last one in stock.

We may not want to accept technology in some areas of our lives, but it does make our lives simpler in many ways. Diane loves her CPA, but she would not have found out about it without reading *Inc.* magazine. She drives by Office Max and Bullock's every day but doesn't go in unless she has a specific need. Could Office Max and Bullock's have reached her through their newspaper ads for the products? No, because she doesn't read the local newspaper.

"Reverse 900" numbers

To find out who your customers or potential customers are, consider offering a cash rebate for filling out a survey or purchasing your products. Large companies do this on a regular basis, so why shouldn't smaller companies and individual entrepreneurs employ the same techniques—which are now considerably lower in price?

Scherers Communications Inc. offers a Cash Back Telephone Coupon whereby callers to an "800" number get instant rebates on their telephone bills for completing a survey or taking advantage of a coupon offer. Contact Steve Harper at 800 356-6161.

Targeting videophiles and other Americans

"People who prefer certain kinds of media are also similar in their demographics and consumer behavior," says Robert Maxwell, vice president for research at Home Box Office, Inc. "Prime-time TV fans and radio listeners are lackluster groups, and newspaper readers are average Americans. The best consumers are movie-goers, book buyers, videophiles, and compact disk buyers." People who share a preference for media are also likely to share preferences for certain products.

Both ad agencies and advertisers are accusing one another of being slow to react to the new media environment, which includes video-on-demand, pay-per-view, video games, and technology that will even recommend an evening's lineup of shows based on a viewer's profile. Edwin L. Artzt, CEO of Proctor & Gamble, said, "We must preserve our ability to use television as our principal advertising medium." Artzt recommended that agencies and clients should use interactive advertising to engage consumers in commercials and provide direct consumer response. The industry should also do more targeting of individual households. "If a family has a newborn baby, we can make sure they get a Pampers commercial."[4]

Newspapers also customize their ads according to their target market. The *New York Times* offers an abridged version with customized ads, delivered by satellite and fax machine to subscribers worldwide. For example, if you're on a cruise ship the ship edition of the *New York TimesFAX* that will be slipped under your cabin door sometimes contains an MCI ad stating, "Save on Calls at Ports of Call—No delays, no need to speak a foreign language, no foreign currencies to deal with, no exchange rates to figure out, no easier, more convenient way to travel from country to country. All vacations should be this ship shape." The ad continues with a list of WorldPhone access numbers and instructions on how to charge the calls to your MasterCard, Visa, or Eurocard if you don't have an MCI card. This is another example of how technology helps target a specific audience not just the mass market.

The box that's challenging MTV

Video Jukebox Network in Miami offers The Box, an interactive television service whereby, in exchange for answering a few questions and paying a $3 charge added to your phone bill, you tell your television what type of programming you want to watch, and when. Dial a "900" number, punch in a three-digit code to select a video and the selected video will be on your TV within twenty minutes.

" . . . The Box is a force to be reckoned with," says Hosh Gureli of KMEL in San Francisco. "It's better than call-out research. It's instantaneous. These people are paying for what they see."

Caller demographic information is immediately available on the five hundred thousand call-in requests each month. "When John Smith calls us from Dubuque, we've got him," says Les Garland, vice president for programming at the network. "We can have a list of 2 million people and tell our advertisers exactly who these people are."[5]

High-tech coupons

Vision Value Network, a joint venture of Procter & Gamble, Dun & Bradstreet, GTE Interactive Services, and others distributes electronic coupons for over 450 brands. As groceries are scanned, a computer at the cash register prints out coupons targeted to the customers most likely to use them. A shopper who buys a diet soft drink will immediately receive a coupon for a low-calorie frozen entree; a person buying baby food might get a coupon for diapers.[6]

Prospecting tools

Statmaster by Computer Easy International and PSearch-USA from Tetrad offer desktop demographics information which can be used with other programs. Public Opinion Survey by Stolzberg Research Inc. creates and analyzes surveys with up to 125 questions and 40 demographic variables.

National Decision Systems by Equifax says their MicroVision customer segmentation is the most innovative ever developed, has been used successfully by the nation's most prosperous companies, and is what others are trying to emulate. Call 800 866-6520 for more information.

Prizm Planner by Claritas/NPDC is an easy-to-use toolkit for helping companies and individual salespeople find their hottest targets. Incorporating the "You are where you live," theory, the Prizm Planner includes: (1) Cluster Snapshops—descriptions of the forty PRIZM Clusters, their demographics, media usage, and lifestyles; (2) Profiles Product Guide—detailed guidelines and instructions for ordering powerful yet inexpensive PRIZM Profiles of your target audience which will help you identify which PRIZM Clusters are your best prospects and where they are located in your trade area; (3) Case Study Tutorial—case studies in direct marketing, media planning, and more; (4) Presentation Manager—slides and script to make you an expert in presenting the Power of PRIZM for consumer targeting; (5) PC software that lets you look up the PRIZM Clusters for any zip code in the United States. To contact PRIZM call 800 234-5973.

Market Statistics offers GeoVALS "The Cluster Buster." Cluster programs would be great if homogeneous zip codes existed. Houses in any given area may look similar, but inside each home very different people reside. Next door to a struggling worker may be an aspiring believer, taking night courses and investing in her own future. Individually, they exhibit significantly different consumer behavior as do many people in neighborhoods across the country. GeoVALS, a joint venture between Market Statistics and SRI International, provides data that allow marketers to better:

- Predict consumer behavior in every zip code
- Identify prime markets
- Measure media audiences
- Allocate advertising resources
- Develop and position new products

SRI's program identifies values and lifestyles based on empirical, primary research obtained from consumers, then describes them as belonging to one of eight groups. They break down every zip code into households.

This geo-demo-psychographic marketing tool helps many diverse industries make significantly better marketing decisions. According to Market Statistics, their GeoVALS system can help you understand consumer values, lifestyles, and geographic densities better than any cluster program. Call 212 592-6246.

The Consumer Research Center was established to help marketers monitor the rapidly changing marketplace. The Center's prime purpose is to keep you tuned in to the who, what, where, and when of consumer buying power and spending patterns. The Consumer Research Center is a division of The Conference Board, a nonprofit business research organization. Among the products and services they offer are *The Consumer Market Guide, A Marketer's Guide to Discretionary Income*, and a two-volume series titled *How Consumers Spend Their Money*. These publications will help you identify your best prospects, formulate advertising campaigns, plan all marketing activities, develop new products, and enter new markets. Call them at 212 339-0303 or fax 212 980-7014.

The U.S. Government Bureau of the Census publishes the Census Catalog and Guide which offers information about thousands of bureau publications on demographic and economic subjects. They exist in print, microfilm and microfiche, compact disc, and computer tape in the Depository Library System (fourteen hundred libraries) and the Census Library System. To find the one closest to you, call your public library or call 301 763-4100 and ask for the Census Catalog and Guide. Or call the Census Bureau's data user services division at 301 763-5820.

Demographics USA offers data on more than sixty data variables for every county, metro area and TV market in the United States. Available in print, diskette, or CD-ROM version, it includes geographic information, demographics, economics and projections, business characteristics, and lifestyles and market potential. Call Market Statistics at 800 685-7828.

S.M.A.R.T.—Strategic Marketing Analysis: Resources & Techniques by *American Demographics*—gives an overview of major consumer trends and shows how to find and use information to predict consumer behavior. S.M.A.R.T. explains how trends in ethnic diversity, household structure, the link between educational attainment and household income, and age distribution will affect the demand for goods and services.

Infomark for Windows is a geographically-based marketing information and applications system for desktop marketing. Just use your "point and click" mouse to define a geographic area of any size or shape, anywhere in the United States. Then quickly access the information you need on people, households, businesses, and competition in your trade area. Greater sales and profits are possible by using Infomark for Windows to perform market analysis, site selection, customer segmentation and targeting, business and competitive analysis, and strategic planning. Call 800 866-6510.

Thomas's Register, a twenty-five volume directory of American manufacturers, is available on CD-ROM. Instant Prospects by Pinpoint Systems has a database of more than sixty-five hundred U.S. companies.

For information on the 1990 Consumer Expenditure Survey, contact the Bureau of Labor Statistics, 600 E. Street, NW (Room 4216), Washington, DC 20212.

JapanSite, a desktop target marketing firm, makes downtown Tokyo only a function key away. JapanSite gives you detailed information on consumers and businesses in Japan, complete data on population, housing, occupation, and business establishments. Call 800 949-9440.

Use a market research service

Claritas Inc. has broken down the entire United States into geodemographic clusters, some as small as three hundred households. Depending on where you live, they can pretty much tell you what kind of car you drive, what magazines you read, and a lot about your tastes. They have identified sixty-two distinct classes, each with its own set of beliefs and aspirations. At the top are the super rich and at the bottom are inner-city single-parent families.

Mediamark Research Inc. (MRI) and Simmons Market Research Bureau (SMRB) combine both the demographic and psychographic characteristics of various media audiences and product or brand purchasers. They look for statistical similarities among the neighboring residents of different types of neighborhoods. By turning to census-based data to find neighborhoods around the entire country populated with similar people, they use "geodemographics" to describe the most prevalent types of consumers in particular areas, right down to individual block groups, based on their original sample of twenty thousand.[7]

Other researchers also place considerable emphasis on where you live. Market researchers can now pinpoint the class status and buying patterns of just about everyone in the U.S. on a neighborhood-by-neighborhood basis. A principal at a Massachusetts research firm called Virtual Media Resources, Josh Ostroff, says "Once I know where you live, I don't need to know a whole lot more about you."[8] Most of us, however, bristle at the thought of being considered the same as our neighbors in attitudes, values, beliefs, and even shopping habits.

R.L. Polk & Co. can provide information to help you identify your best prospects, reach new markets, plan inventories, choose the most viable retail sites, and even predict consumer buying trends. Polk's unique resources provide information relating to motor vehicles, lifestyles, demographics, neighborhoods, businesses, geography, and purchasing behavior. They will tailor this information to meet your specific needs and help you interpret the information.

Donnelley Marketing's database includes the buying patterns and habits of 87 million households. In exchange for filling out a form on household spending, they send coupons and money-saving offers. Companies can ask for their own particular questions to meet their marketing needs and direct their efforts to those consumers they identify as most likely to buy their product.[9]

These and other groupings are analyzed in-depth by professional marketing services using procedures worthy of military intelligence gathering. Buying habits, liquid assets, investments, and other criteria are pieced together to produce a multifaceted portrait of the customer. This enables sales and marketing people to pursue "planned penetration based on potential," which depends on fluid information such as projected change in income. Conventional data gleaned from averaging zip code areas and the like are no longer enough. House-to-house statistics are the new standard.[10]

Direct mail companies are among the most aggressive clients for this sort of research. Such enterprises sent out 13.5 billion catalogs last year, accounting for more than $50 billion in sales, and much of their success is due to knowing which addresses are populated by Lands' End types and which by L.L. Beanies.[11] According to a Direct Marketing Association 1990 survey, 64 percent of all companies use demographic overlays to improve response to customer mailings.[12]

Remember the human element

Even with all the technology available today, the human touch should never be forgotten. Salespeople will probably always know more about their target customers than the databases. There are some things a salesperson in the field can do that a database can never duplicate. But the databases can provide more decision-making information than individual salespeople.

Additional resources:

CACI	800 292-2224
Donnelley	800 866-2255
Metromail Corp.	800 666-6245
NDS/Equifax	800 877-5560
R.L. Polk & Co.	313 292-3200
TRW Marketing	800 527-3933
American Demographics:	
Software:	800 828-1133
Products/Services	800 828-1133
Marketing Tools Magazine	800 828-1133

Advertising Research Foundation
641 Lexington Avenue
New York, NY 10022

Chapter 6

The Incredible Shrinking Machine
(CD-ROM)

"CD-ROMS make floppy disks look like Post-It notes."
— Dan Gutman

If you want to take a ride on the information highway's fast lane, take a spin on a CD-ROM (compact disk read-only memory). The little machines the size of a cigar box are exactly like the ones you're using to play your favorite music, but can turn your computer into a powerful information base or put a database in your briefcase. This technology places huge amounts of searchable data at your fingertips.

A single compact disk can store 680 megabytes of audio-visual information (seven hundred times as much as a floppy disk) which is equivalent to two hundred thousand typed pages or a twenty-five volume set of encyclopedias with sound and pictures.

A chief advantage of the CD-ROM format is its low cost and space-saving feature. You can carry an electronic library with you and call it up on your laptop computer. The data is integrated on a digital format, allowing for cutting and pasting directly into an existing word processing file. It's faster and less expensive than manual research. It's also much cheaper than on-line charges.

What do CD-ROMs have to do with selling?

CD-ROMS have every conceivable database available for direct mail or one-on-one selling. List companies offer millions of consumer or business names by every category. Some will screen out unneeded information or customize lists. With this technology it's much easier to turn prospects into customers by using it for:

- Market research and planning—develop more effective sales and marketing strategies, determine what types of industries to sell to, what geographic markets to target, and identify prospects in those markets.

- Advertising and media appraisals—Standard Rate and Data Service puts its business and consumer magazine directories on compact disks. Media buyers can obtain circulation numbers, reader demographics, and ad size specifications in a menu format. BMW of North America put out a CD-ROM press release to auto journalists to demonstrate its all-season traction system.

- Site and sales territory evaluation—determine the best locations and size of potential markets, then map out itineraries and routes which will deploy your sales force more effectively.

- Lead generation—identify high-potential prospects and provide timely information to your sales force and distributors.

- Direct mail—target exactly the right markets and make your mailings more responsive with key decision-makers' names.

- Telemarketing—identify the right prospects to call and let the software do the dialing for you.

- Locating suppliers—not only can you locate prospects, but you can find out about companies you might want to do business with for both corporate and personal needs.

Why flip your floppies for CDs?

Numerous companies including 3M are now putting their catalogs on CD-ROM and others will soon follow suit. Whirlpool uses a CD-ROM for its repair manual. McDonald's uses them for training guides. Oracle Software Company put its 1993 annual report on a CD-ROM.[1] General Motors puts its parts prices on CD-ROM for its dealers.

If you're staying at the Marriott in Santa Clara, California, check out InfoTravel, a Yellow Pages on CD-ROM. You can check out 175 local and national advertisers including hotel services, restaurants, entertainment and sight-seeing options, maps, or shop from your room. If you want to make dinner reservations, just press a button on the remote control and not only will you have the maitre'd on the line, but he will know who's calling.

Mark Heyer of HeyerTech Inc., a Palo Alto firm specializing in custom system design and image databases, helped The Gap create a digital database for its advertising. In the past they had stored their print advertising in portfolios. With thousands of old ads on file, Gap staff had to plow through tons of paper to locate a particular piece. Materials frequently got lost in the shuffle. Now, everything is on laser disc, where it's easy to access and print with a computer.

According to Heyer, digital technology may find similar applications in other Gap departments. "The merchandisers told us that the storage of clothing samples was a major problem, since they create seven seasons a year and can't store more than three seasons' worth on site. If all the samples were archived in a (digital) system, designers could easily go back and research previous styles."[2]

Several mail order companies are putting their catalogs on CD. Let's say you're interested in a raincoat. With a click you'll see a listing of all the catalog companies on the CD that carry raincoats. Check the companies you're interested in and look at the raincoats each of them offers. If you want to know the fabric content or whether or not the lining can be unzipped, click again for additional information. When you find the item you want, you can order it over your computer modem and, in some areas, by cable.

The National Association of Home Builders has an electronic Buyer's Guide for home building products on CD-ROM that includes everything, including the kitchen sink. You'll not only see all of the styles a manufacturer makes, but you'll even find out what distributor carries the product you need.

Best of all, the CD-ROM catalog is interactive: You can tell it what you want and find information quickly and logically. If you're looking for a kitchen sink, aim your cursor at "fixtures" and click. An alphabetical list of manufacturers will appear. Move the cursor to the company name you want to check out, and click. The catalog's table of contents will appear. Click on the symbol for sinks. Three images will appear on the screen; one each for enameled cast iron, stainless steel, and acrylic. Click on one of the three sinks and you'll get the product page for that particular sink, showing the sink and its specs. From there you can click on a "color" button to see the colors available for that sink, or click on the faucet holes in the sink photo to bring compatible faucet models up on the screen.

Some companies include videos highlighting the features of their products, and some show their entire catalog—from color images to spec sheets. If a company has included its full catalog, you can call it up on the screen, select a product, and review its specs, all in a matter of seconds. Available for $29.95, call 202 452-0800.[3]

Lights, Camera, Manual!

Home brewing a multimedia CD-ROM is not for the faint-hearted, but it can be done. Just as desktop publishing brought a lot of art and design work back in-house, a lot of the production of interactive media will be done in-house. A master-making machine is around $6,000. The discs costs about $1 to manufacture.

In an article explaining how it can be done, David Churbuck says, "Your patience and pocketbook may never be the same, but with any luck you will wind up with something easier to look at, and much easier to carry around, than the usual stack of paper flip charts and carousel of 35 mm slides."

If you want a good overview on how to create your own multimedia CD-ROM, read Churbuck's article "Lights! Camera! Manual!" in the January 17, 1994 issue of *Forbes* and "Show and Tell" by Dennis James in the May 1993 issue of *Success*.

Window shopping for CD-ROMs

American Business Information Inc. offers a database software program called Business America-ON DISC for anyone who sells to businesses, which empowers salespeople with information on more than 10 million publicly and privately owned companies. Rather than searching through phone books or buying lists, this software allows you to select prospects by geographic areas, company name, type of business, number of employees, sales volume, and decision-makers' titles.

The Official Phonedisc by The Database America Company provides names, addresses, and phone numbers for 9.5 million U.S. businesses and can be called up by type of business, company name, address, or phone number. All this costs under $100.

Database America and Digital Directory Assistance joined forces and created PhoneDisc USA Business which provides names, addresses, and phone numbers for 90 million Americans and over 10 million businesses. Companies can be found by name, address, phone number, 4-digit Standard Industry Code (SIC), and other options. Call 800 223-7777, or 201 476-2300 if you live in New Jersey.

Allegro New-Media offers a multimedia reference to America's top companies. Business 500 has comprehensive information on five hundred major U.S. companies plus interactive videos for $49.95. Business Library contains the complete text of twelve top business reference books for $59.95. For the dealer closest to you, call 201 808-1992.

If you're interested in buying or selling property in California, contact DATAQUICK at 619 455-6900. They offer California on CD so you can instantly access complete sale/loan, ownership and assessment information on every property in forty-eight counties and assessors plat maps in thirty counties. It can be used to identify insurance prospects, target loan or refinancing prospects and customize telemarketing and direct mail lists. CDs are also available for Arizona, Nevada, Oregon, and Washington.

Transamerica Information Management Services' MetroScan brings salespeople, marketers, and other professionals immediate, inexpensive access to databases of public record information from the county assessor and other public agencies. It includes current sales, sales history, telephone numbers, parcel maps, geo-coded data, census tract data, and other significant information. Hundreds of documents are accessible in seconds, offering greater speed and accuracy than microfiche. As a sales professional you can identify your prospecting area on the digitized map, have the names and addresses of everyone in the area, and create mailing labels or postcards in minutes. For more information call 800 825-7226.

Ask your local computer supermarket about shareware. Fourteen hundred business programs are available on one CD for $10. Another one offers fifteen hundred programs for $15.

Also look into MarketPlace Business from Market Place Information Corporation and DIALOG ONDISC from DIALOG Information Services, Inc., and The National Yellow Pages Directory which has millions of entries on four CDs. Accumail will give you zip codes for every area plus mailing information. *Thomas's Register* is the equivalent of a twenty-five-volume directory of American manufacturers available on CD-ROM.

Print Shop Deluxe CD Ensemble (Broderbund, $69.95) offers fonts, graphics, text effects, layouts, etc. for creating letterhead, brochures, mailouts, and other sales materials.

Corel Gallery (Corel, $59) offers ten thousand clip art images, six thousand of which are in color, for both PC and Macintosh to make your Print Shop creations look snazzy.

Lost and found

On a sales call and can't find your destination? Your CD-ROM will give you a map of every block in the United States.

Check out the DeLorme Street Atlas U.S.A. for $169. If you're making a sales call in an unfamiliar city and trying to locate your client, put their phone number into your database and within seconds the street map of their location will be displayed on your computer screen. You can check on restaurants, hotels, customers, and suppliers. Let's say you're on a business trip and want to take home a gift to your kids. Use your CD-ROM software and you can locate all the toy stores in your area. Or better yet, locate the computer stores and buy them some new educational software.

Automap Pro ($250) by Automap Inc. will plot your business call from door to door, based on your input regarding how fast you want to go, type of road, and other criteria. Plug in your list of sales calls you need to make for the day and the program will recommend the best itinerary and allow you to link up database information on each client.

Are you going on a business trip to Europe and you've never been there before? Go buy a CD on traveling by car through Europe so that when you're actually there, everything will feel like déjà vu.

Library on a disc

Microsoft offers a portable reference library containing *The Concise Columbia Encyclopedia, The American Heritage Dictionary, Roget's Thesaurus, Bartlett's Familiar Quotations, Hammond Atlas,* and the *World Almanac and Book of Facts.* The 1993 edition included audio clips, animation, music, and digitized photos in addition to text.

Microsoft also publishes an encyclopedia called *Encarta.* If you're writing a thank-you note or sales letter to a client, look in your vast library on your CD-ROM and find just the right quote to customize the correspondence.

Gale Directory of Databases lists nearly all the choices of databases and can be found at the library or by calling 800 347-4253. If your collection becomes very big, you'll need Fetch, a cataloging, browsing, and retrieval tool from Aldus. In seconds Fetch can search thousands of files anywhere on your floppies and CD-ROMs. Items can be copied, previewed, played, printed, or placed in your presentation software.

Soon the Vatican Library of more than 1 million books will be on CD-ROM. This includes eight thousand published during the first fifty years of the printing press. IBM plans to convert the

Vatican's pre-1985 catalog of nearly 2 million cards into an electronic database reachable on Internet, the global computer network. IBM will work with the library and Pontifical University of Rio de Janeiro in Brazil.[4]

Need help?

Want to get information on a business-related topic for your client? Just check out your CD-ROM. Without a CD-ROM you won't be able to take advantage of the best computing has to offer a salesperson.

CD-ROMs in Print lists six thousand CDs on census data, demographic statistics, geographical mapping, advertising, general marketing, and telephone and mailing lists. It can be ordered from Meckler Media, 11 Ferry Lane West, Westport, CT 06880; 203 226-6967.

Multi-media magazines

Magazines are also available on CD-ROM format. Cowles Business Media created *Open* and *Open Wider*, interactive magazines incorporating full-motion video, hypertext, animation, music, and many other illustrations not included in the printed magazine. You can catch up on your reading while on the road with your laptop. Or if you want to wander through an art museum, watch music videos, play computer games, or study the encyclopedia, just put in the appropriate CD.

An interactive multimedia magazine called *Nautilus* is published exclusively on CD-ROM. For $11 a month, subscribers receive a disk with twenty hours of content on it. Designed for browsing, it's a mix of articles, photos, music, and video, with a heavy dose of software product samples and hardware reviews. It marries the audiovisual power of a television set to the page-flipping convenience of a printed magazine. If a browser sees an article about Windham Hill singer/ guitarist John Gorka, with a click of a switch he can hear a song from his latest album.[5]

A quarterly children's magazine called *Kidsoft* combines printed articles with a CD-ROM game sampler. After trying out the game, they can purchase it on-line if they like it.[6]

Testdrive a CD-ROM

If you want to try before you buy, call 800 788-8055 and sign up. You will receive a CD-ROM with up to one hundred complete software programs on it that you can try before you buy, so you won't be disappointed with the real thing. Okay, admit it. Your larcenous side is asking, if I have the program, why buy it? Because some technological genius programmed the software with a counter so it only runs a limited number of times. After you reach your limit you can dial an "800" number and give them a credit card number. In turn they will give you a code that disables the counter.

Several portable CD-ROM drives are on the market ranging in price from $300 to $600. Notebook CD-ROM computers begin at about $3,000. Computer companies say 40 percent of home personal computer buyers are purchasing CD-ROM drives. Five million were sold in 1993 and they predict 11 million will be sold in 1994. Blockbuster Video is experimenting with CD-ROM rentals.

Multimedia personal computers cost between $1,500 and $3,500. If you have a computer with at least a 386 microprocessor, you can upgrade for CD-ROM. Software is written for DOS, Windows, Macintosh, MPS (Multimedia standard), or a combination of these. You'll need an internal or external CD-ROM drive ($300-$900), interface or drive controller ($30-$400), sound card ($70-$1,000), and speakers ($15 to $300). These add-on components are available separately or in a kit ($500-$1,000).

Home Office magazine surveyed its readers and found that 15 percent owned a CD drive. Sixty-one percent plan to buy one soon. In 1993 thirty-five hundred software programs were available on CD-ROM and manufacturers expect to have forty-five hundred out by the end of 1994, with total sales of $100 million. It costs manufacturers about one-third as much to manufacture a CD-ROM disk as it does to manufacture a set of floppy diskettes containing the same data. CDs cannot be erased and can't be copied without expensive equipment. Although it costs about $1 to make a CD, they range in price from about $20 to several hundred dollars, but as more titles come out and the volume increases, the price is expected to come down to the price of music CDs.

Many of the new computers come equipped with CD-ROM drives built in. If you're buying an IBM compatible computer, get one with a Zero Insertion Force socket which will accept Pentium chips that can do parallel processing, or more than one task at a time. The best way to use CDs on PCs is with Microsoft Windows. It allows you to open a window and search a CD for information without shutting down whatever else you're doing.

Coming soon to a phone or TV near you is CD access through your cable or phone company. You can call up the information you need and peruse through it on a use charge or download it to a reusable high-storage device called a magneto-optical drive which will hold about sixty thousand pages.

CD-ROM players are available for both computers and televisions and the quality of the finished product is about the same. The only obvious difference is the keyboard in front of the computer. According to Jonathan Epstein, publisher of *Multimedia World*, a magazine devoted to PC-based multimedia, "There are 6 1/2 million CD-ROM players attached to something out there. About 5 1/2 million are connected to PCs." Television CD-ROMs are better for entertainment while computer-based CD systems are better for information-retrieval and education, displaying text, and storing information.

A chief disadvantage of the CD-ROM is that it's not possible to record new information onto a compact disk without a mastering machine. Once a read/write disk is perfected it will revolutionize the medium.

If you've been waiting for a good reason to buy a computer, or to add a CD-ROM drive to your system, this is it. Knowledge is not only power, but in selling it means wealth and advancement. Never before has no much information been available in such a small format. Your competitors are buying computers and your customers are beginning to expect them. Don't be the last one on your block to own one.

Chapter 7

Seeing Is Believing
(Multimedia)

"Multimedia combines the audiovisual power of the television, the publishing power of the printing press, and the interactive power of the computer."

—Daniel Burrus[1]

Ric Adams and John McCoy are salesmen at different ends of the technology spectrum. Ric Adams sells an auto polishing system and uses an eight-year-old twenty-two-pound pet ape named Alex to guarantee getting in to see auto dealers. John McCoy sells multimedia productions for Ikonic Interactive and can pop an interactive diskette into a computer and demonstrate his product with video, sophisticated color graphics, photos and music on 16-bit stereo sound.

Although both salesmen use totally different presentation techniques and are at opposite ends of the technology spectrum, they both have an understanding of consumer behavior and what it takes to get someone's attention and make a point.

Not many people use pet apes as part of their presentation like Ric Adams does, but more and more companies are turning to multimedia presentations to reach their customers. Before a company is sold on it, they need to understand how it will help their business.

Bandag Inc., one of the world's largest manufacturers of commercial tire-retreading systems based in Muscatine, Iowa, wanted five interactive kiosks for its international conference in Maui, Hawaii. They contracted with Ikonic Interactive to promote their Total Quality Management program, to introduce their new product line, to explain the bottom-line impact of new warranty and inventory control programs, and to keep attendees informed about all the events planned for the ten-day conference.

Jim Cook, Bandag's creative director, explained, "We have the latest state-of-the-art technology in our industry, so it was appropriate that we used state-of-the-art for education at our conference." Of course, they also wanted the kiosks to be appealing to non-computer users.

To achieve this, Ikonic developed an interface in which all navigation choices are visible on the screen at any one time. They also created video portraits of the members of the convention, digitized them, and overnight created QuickTime movies. The next day, the QuickTime video impressions were available throughout the convention at the push of a button on five touchscreen monitors. Ikonic used video, Macintosh animation, and QuickTime as key elements in the interactive exhibits. For a more detailed explanation of the equipment and how it was done to the clients satisfaction and delight, see *MacWeek*, 05.04.92 Volume 6 Number 18.

Aetna Life & Casualty Co. has been using multimedia to add sizzle to major corporate presentations. Hughes Aircraft developed an interactive kiosk for its corporate parent, General Motors; on display at Epcot Center, the kiosk allowed GM to track the popularity of various cars and trucks. And Bethlehem Steel Corp. developed an interactive training program on computer applications in steel manufacturing that turned out to be a valuable marketing tool as well.[2]

Multimedia is not necessarily a new technology, but rather a way of thinking about information. Robert May, founder and president of Ikonic Interactive, which has developed multimedia projects for such clients as Apple Computer, Time-Warner, Sony Corp. of America and Pacific Bell, concurs and adds that multimedia is indeed a new way of looking at information, and it's enhancing the value of the information itself.

May predicts that "people will be selling information by the pound," creating new business opportunities. "It's possible that the market research you did last year has value to people in non-competing industries," he points out. "Everybody has information to sell. Don't wait. Leverage your information assets now. Think about what you have and how to package it."[3]

What is multimedia?

First we say you have to own a computer, then we tell you to purchase a CD-ROM, now we say you just can't live without multimedia. What is it anyway? And most importantly, what does it have to do with sales?

Don't feel isolated if you don't quite understand it all. Francy Blackwood, a high-tech reporter who covers the multimedia market in San Francisco, says, "Despite a recent flood of press coverage hyping the digital revolution, interactive multimedia remains as foreign and unfathomable to most people as the conflict in Bosnia and Herzegovina."[4] Feel better now?

A multimedia kit consists of a CD-ROM disk drive and a sound board, which is a board installed into your computer to give you better music, voice, animation, and sound-effect production from the CDs than an older or less elaborate computer provides. Many new computers have multimedia kits built in.

In his book *TechnoTrends*, Daniel Burrus states, "By blending personal computers with either digital video interactive (DVI) or CD-ROM based storage systems, you can create the foundation for an interactive system that integrates data, sound, and video." He recommends four application areas for multimedia:

a.   business presentations

b.   training and education

c.   reference database

d.   electronic correspondence[5]

According to Robert May, there's a massive market out there. When asked what businesses need that multimedia can provide, he stated that training is probably the most robust application, but the list of business applications for multimedia include sales and marketing tools, electronic brochures, marketing presentations that run on laptop computers, and interactive kiosks, which are often used in trade show marketing.

"What interactive multimedia does best is to transform the content of information," May stated in another interview. "Content transformation adds to the value of media integration. There is a definite shift in the value of information when it is made interactive."

Dave Miller, a San Francisco multimedia marketing consultant, says, "The thing that will make multimedia successful is the interactivity, the aspect that makes it different from multiple media as it exists now." The interactive component of multimedia gives the user immediate feedback and control of information, and in that sense, "it's an incredible teaching tool," he says.[6]

John McCoy considers himself more of an educator than a salesman. When making cold calls for Ikonic, he frequently uses this statement: "We're producers of interactive multimedia. It's a new generation of strategic communications, and a lot of companies are looking into it. I'd like to let you know what we do, and what's going on in the industry."[7]

What *is* going on in the industry? Research and consulting firm Information Workstation Group of Alexandria, Virginia, predicts that by 1995, commercial applications of multimedia will generate $6.9 billion in volume. May predicts "This industry will be measured in tens of billions of dollars within ten years, and will fundamentally change the relationship people have with information."

According to *California Business*, San Francisco ranks number one as the center of digital companies specializing in multimedia. A task force at the San Francisco Chamber of Commerce is marketing the city as a multimedia center and has a goal of providing a link between multimedia developers and the local business community.

How does multimedia happen and is it something you will be doing soon? Before we get into the details for you techies out there, let's backtrack to consider the reasons why presentations are an important sales tool and start by learning how to do simple ones.

Why do a visual presentation?

Miles Busby, president of Source Technologies, now laughs about his first sales call on GE. At the time it seemed like the end of his career. First, he accidentally jammed an automatic door, closing down shipping operations for the entire day. Then, when his demo printer failed, GE lost three days' worth of production orders and had to hire a data-entry person to enter them. Undaunted, Busby returned but still couldn't get the equipment to work. "After that," he says, "I was too embarrassed to go back."[8]

If you have a similar story to tell, you know the importance of a smooth presentation.

The whole object of a presentation is communication. Salespeople need to take their customers through all five steps of the information processing procedure:

1. Exposure
2. Attention
3. Comprehension
4. Acceptance
5. Retention[9]

Customers must pay attention long enough for the desired action to happen and then remember what information was given. Creating a dynamic visual presentation can make an enormous difference in the customer's retention and your increased productivity. The retention factor for remembering new information only twenty-four hours after exposure is about 10 percent of what one reads, 20 percent of what one hears, 30 percent of what one sees, and 65 percent of what one sees and hears.

Don't be afraid to repeat your message over and over to help the client retain the information. However, don't depend on your visual presentation to do your job. It can only augment your personal effectiveness, not take the place of it.

Ten years ago most sales professionals rarely used visual presentations. When the situation called for a presentation such as a seminar or high ticket group sale, overhead projectors, slide projectors, or a video set-up were the choices. Now, you can

101

create a slide presentation on your computer, load it into your laptop and carry it to be viewed by your client to augment your sales presentation. With the click of a mouse you can not only show color charts of company and product sales, but pictures of the product, testimonials from happy customers, and important benefits of the product. All this comes with music, moving images, sound, and interactive involvement if you choose.

A presentation can be customized for each client, taking as little as fifteen minutes to make the changes on your computer. You can also create professional personalized handouts or brochures in color on your word-processing or desktop publishing software and print them on your laser printer. If you don't have color you can take it to a print shop and let them run it on their color printer.

Gay Chappell, brand manager for SuperMac's business productivity products, says "Visual sales presentations have been the key to unlocking our customers' purchasing power . . . Presentation products can turn any salesperson into a sales dynamo."

Now that you know what it is and why you should use it, let's look at how. It all starts with the right software.

Choosing your software

A WordPerfect Presentations from Windows ad reads: "It's 3 A.M. You've lost your appetite. You've lost your confidence. One more mediocre presentation and you could lose your client. Clearly, this is no time for a pile of handouts and a few lame jokes." Another ad features a paper napkin with scribbles all over it and reads, "OK. The presentation looks great. On a napkin. But you can't pass that around a boardroom. Now you're stuck. You can't draw. You can't paint. And faking a heart attack is out of the question." WordPerfect Presentations for Windows is the most comprehensive software of its kind. With it creating attention-getting presentations with overheads, 3-D charting, slides, sound, and video clips is simple. And no other major presentation package comes with more clip art images or lets you scan and customize your own. So you have the power to save the day, not to mention your reputation. For a free test drive kit call 800 526-3849.

Presentation software breaks down into four categories:

- Traditional slideshow–oriented products
- Multimedia programs that add frame-by-frame animation
- Collections of multimedia add-ons, such as sound, graphics, and images
- Programs that catalog and locate items from those collections[10]

The three most used software products are Aldus Persuasion 2.1, Microsoft Power Point 3.0, and Lotus Development's Freelance Graphics. All three packages are $495, all available for either Mac or Windows users.

These programs cover the entire still presentation. You start with an outline, so you can map your presentation slide by slide, add the usual text, and use graphic tools to make charts and graphs. Plus you can design and create individual slides, overhead transparencies, 35mm slides, and notes.[11]

You can upgrade your presentations with software programs that add movement and sound. Check out Interactive Media Corp. Special Delivery for $399 and Macromedia's Director ($1,195) and Action ($495).

If you already have a top-of-the-line word processor such as Microsoft Word or WordPerfect (each $495), you can design presentation outlines for dynamic presentations with tables, charts, or graphs. A step up in terms of graphics ability is Aldus's Pagemaker, a popular desktop publishing product which creates visuals automatically carried through on each page.

Sound complicated? Actually it's fun once you get into it. Let's take Aldus Persuasion for example: The tutorial will demonstrate how it's done and even walk you through an interesting simple slide show. You can choose auto templates to adjust and enhance to suit your objective. You can create a chart and data sheet, plot it, shade it, use textures, patterns, and line styles. You can add a graphic or visual to help make your point. Drawing tools let you make any shape yourself or import computer-drawn images into your show. The computer will show you automatic features which add emphasis, clarity, and movement. You can create charts with drama, choosing from two hundred colors. Even with a black and white monitor you can designate colors. You can produce your own vibrant, alive, full-scale slide show for presentation on a slide projector or computer.

Varitronics offers a work station that's designed to create presentation charts. The Presentation Station links their Poster-Printer Plus with your PC or Macintosh computer. Create your chart on screen and print it on their special printer to create a twenty-three by thirty-inch presentation chart or poster. The system includes software and is compatible with other software packages. For a free demonstration disk call 800 637-5461.

You can turn your ordinary slide projector into a computer-based presentation system with a portable system that fits in the palm of your hand. Call 800 983-6060.

Enhancing Presentations

CD-ROM disks can add any information you can imagine to your presentation (see Chapter 6 on CD-ROMs) both for static (slide) and multimedia. From CDs you can access clip art, high-resolution stock photography, animation, and even video footage and add them to your presentations to get your points across.

Most of the databases are found on CD-ROMs so you must have the computer hardware available to pull it out and the software to bring it into your presentation.

If you are confused on where to find database information to add facts, figures, and graphics to your presentation, you could "info surf," meaning searching through dozens of different sources trying to find the database which suits you. You could go to the library and look at Gale Directory of Databases or purchase it. (Gale, 800 347-4253, $280).

Explore specific software to suit your purpose. Designs can be customized or examples made in advance. Search journals and articles specific to your client to take with you to present on your laptop to the client.

Check out Compact Disclosure from Disclosure Inc. and HealthPLAN-CD from Silver-Platter Information, Inc.

Fetch, the cataloging, browsing, and retrieval tool from Aldus, can search thousands of files anywhere on your floppies and CD-ROMs in seconds. Items can be copied, previewed, played, printed, or placed in your presentation software.[12]

Scanners—separate tools available in several sizes—are needed to "scan" your company logo, picture of the president, and other personal or custom or original graphics not available on CD-ROMs.

Scanners do just that, scan the image on a hard copy onto your disk or drive to place into your presentation or handout. Hand-held color scanners for small images can be purchased from $250. A color flat-bed scanner works more conveniently. They run from $800 to $1,500 depending on how much resolution and size of document needed.

Adding Multimedia

To add the depth of a full-fledged multimedia presentation containing movement and sound, you need multimedia products such as Macromedia's Director ($1,195.00), Action ($495), or Interactive Media Corp's Special Delivery ($399). "These programs add movement and sound to your presentations. You have an automated log that sweeps across the screen, accompanied by the roar of a jet airplane or the crash of symbols. Use on-screen buttons and menus to hop anywhere in your presentation."[13]

WordPerfect Presentations for Windows on the PC offers comprehensive software to create presentations with overheads, 3-D charting, slides, sound, and video clips—or lets you scan and customize your own. (WordPerfect Presentations, 800 526-3849).

IBM Storyboard LIVE! allows you to add animation.

Showing off your show

If you anticipate several people sitting in on the demonstration instead of just one or two, use an nVIEW MediaPro LCD display panel that will fit on an overhead projector. Everything you're doing on your notebook computer will then show up on a big screen.

Your notebook computer will function like a mainframe terminal if you use a modem and Attachmate EXTRA! for

Windows. You will be able to switch from PC to mainframe programs and send files back and forth from a customer's location. When the customer asks about something you hadn't anticipated, you can access your mainframe back at the office and in just a few seconds produce a graphic or chart in the customer's office using your portable printer.

Scared of do-it-yourself? Hire the pros

Ikonic Interactive of San Francisco wants to help businesses seeking a competitive advantage in the international marketplace. The company specializes in large, technically complex projects which typically require integration of databases, analog and/or digital video, custom code, and strong design and project management skills. Ikonic is a certified software developer for Apple Computer, the Sony Multimedia CD-ROM player, and MacroMedia; it is also an IBM Multimedia Business Partner. Selected clients include Time-Warner, Sony Corporation of America, Dow Jones & Company, Apple Computer, Boeing, Intel, NEC, Pacific Bell, Panasonic, Paramount Communications, Taligent, WordPerfect, Inc. Magazine, and others. Call John McCoy at 415 864-3200.

R.R. Donnelley & Sons Company believe they can dramatically increase your sales by digitizing and rearranging your sales presentation, training programs, or company catalog on interactive multimedia. Call 800 438-0223 for a CD-ROM demonstration or a brochure.

California Business published a list of the top one hundred companies in the "Digital Pack." If you want more information about other companies and their services, contact them at 221 Main St., Suite 700, San Francisco, CA 94105 or fax 415 543-8232.

And by the way—remember Ric Adams and John McCoy from the beginning of the chapter? Both of them go on the road with their presentation materials. McCoy's equipment and sample diskettes fit neatly into his computer carrying cases. Adams, on the other hand, frequently faces serious challenges when flying with Alex the simian.

On one trip, Adams and a friend each carried several stuffed animals, disguising the fact that comingled in was Alex, an eight-year-old gibbon. Just when they thought they were home free, the security guard insisted all the toys be run through the x-ray machine. When Ric Adams handed the live ape to the guard and said, "Here, you try running him through that machine," the trip was aborted.

His most successful ploy was buying an airline ticket from Phoenix to Minneapolis for Alex Adams, sedating the ape, wrapping him up in a blanket and boarding before the other passengers because he was carrying a "baby." When the sedative wore off, Adams strapped Alex into his seat and hoped he'd sit still so the flight attendant would think he was a stuffed animal. All went well until lunch was served—Alex reached up and grabbed some of the food. "My God, he's alive!" the attendant screamed.

The captain wasn't impressed with the $431 round-trip ticket Adams had purchased for Alex, but once a plane is in the air it won't turn around even if there *is* a live ape in the cabin. Adams and Alex's high-flying antics made front-page headlines in Minneapolis. Talk about free publicity!

Unfortunately, however, when they tried to use the return portion of their tickets they were in big trouble. Why couldn't he fly as baggage? Would you send your computer as baggage? No way. Besides that, in the extreme heat of the summer most airlines refuse to fly cargo animals into Phoenix.

We're not recommending you emulate Ric Adams' presentation techniques. We are recommending, however, if you aren't already using them, that you learn more about interactive multimedia presentations and how they will help you service your customers. Take the advice of Dennis James, who says, "Other sales reps are walking into your customers' offices with laptops under their arms—and walking away with orders. And if they're not, here's your chance to get ahead of them. Because, sooner or later, they will all be tapping this powerful sales tool."[14]

Chapter 8

E-mail or *EEEK* Mail?
(Electronic Mail)

"Faster than faxing and cheaper than phones, electronic mail is changing the face of customer service."

—Phaedra Hise

Jim Jeter, an account executive with the health care information systems division of Hewlett-Packard's medical products group, credits E-mail with helping him land the biggest sale of his career. Jeter sells HP computer systems to hospitals, managed-care facilities, and doctors' offices by forming partnerships with independent software vendors that provide specialized software programs for practice management, patient accounting, and patient care in hospitals.

Jeter was trying to land a contract to design and install an information system for a group of fourteen hospitals. The competition was fierce. He knew he had to demonstrate Hewlett-Packard's ability to service the customer's needs.

With sales of this size, HP salespeople and managers communicate using special guidelines they call "the big deal process." These guidelines are meant to ensure that each person involved is familiar with every aspect of the sale and has access to up-to-the-minute information. Each team member needed to be available to provide information and keep abreast of all significant developments during the sales cycle, even though they were scattered across the world. Delays in supplying answers would reflect poorly on HP's ability to perform as a vendor.

Jeter relied on Hewlett Packard's internal E-mail system to keep the team connected throughout the sales cycle. Using HP OpenMail which connects HP employees around the world, Jeter formed a distribution group which included his Pittsburgh manager and various product managers who had responsibility for different aspects of the sale.

Jeter created his reports on AmiPro for Windows and sent copies of appropriate documents to his distribution list for approval before he sent it to his customer. His colleagues could approve, correct, or comment on the documents within hours, allowing Jeter to show the customer HP's responsiveness. When sending E-mail Jeter backs it up with voice mail, knowing that most people check their voice-mail more often than their E-mail.

Regularly checking his E-mail for new-product announcements, changes in price or product specifications, company and industry news, or analyses of competitors' products, Jeter stayed on top of all aspects of the bid.

"It's no fun to walk into the office of a customer who has more up-to-date information about your company's products than you do," he says. "With this system, that never happens."

After a two-year sales cycle, Jeter made the sale. "It's almost impossible to land an opportunity like this unless everything goes right," he said. "It helps to have a communications system that helps make that happen."

Jeter also uses his E-mail system to tap hundreds of electronic presentations, ranging from an overview of HP's medical products group to detailed presentations on specific products. He can select the presentation he wants, download it from the E-mail system, modify it and create a customized presentation.[1]

What in the cyberworld is E-mail?

Sealed and delivered by computer, electronic mail, or E-mail, is the transmission of memos and messages over a computer network to another computer or a fax machine. It allows one individual to create a memo, letter, or message and send it to someone else on the system, whether they are sitting at the next desk or around the world. All you need is a personal computer with modem, the software, and an on-line service. Computer users are considered "on-line" when they are connected interactively with other computers or computer networks. E-mail's advantages are speed and around-the-clock responses. And if you want a hard copy, make a copy on your printer or fax.

E-mail combines the depth of a detailed letter or report with the expediency of a phone call, say its proponents, who refer to the U.S. Postal Service as "snail mail." Although E-mail doesn't provide the immediacy of a phone call, a majority of phone calls can be replaced by E-mail without scheduling calls to adjust for different time zones around the world. When traveling, E-mail can be sent and received from virtually anywhere in the world where there is a phone line or a wireless communications area. The messages are stored until your computer is turned on and they are accessible at your convenience, rather than at someone else's convenience as phone calls are. Although it will never supplant the phone, fax machine or Postal Service, it has become the preferred communication tool for E-mail disciples worldwide.

According to the Electronic Mail Association (EMA) in Arlington, Virginia, the use of E-mail among the Fortune 2000, America's largest companies, grew 83 percent between 1991 and 1993. They estimate that 60 million people will be E-mailable by the end of 1994. More than one third of Fortune 2000 company sites use Electronic mail, and new applications are being found for it every day.

How to E-mail like a pro

Electronic mail is ideally suited for use in sales, where immediacy and responsiveness often yield a big competitive advantage. Here are some ways *Selling* magazine's George W. Colombo suggests salespeople can make the most of E-mail.

- Break your paper fixation—the only thing you can do with a paper document is read it. Electronic mail can be modified, edited, forwarded, and easily incorporated into almost any kind of computer-generated document. If your manager sends you three paragraphs via E-mail to add to a proposal, they won't need to be retyped. Electronic mail can be faster and more flexible than paper communications.

- Tap your inner power—you can broadcast an E-mail message throughout permanent or temporary "distribution groups" with a couple of keystrokes, instantly tapping the expertise of far-flung colleagues. There was one salesperson who, to help clinch a deal, turned to his company's E-mail system as a way to locate an existing customer who used the company's product in a specialized way. Within hours he received a name that he could use as a referral. Through traditional channels, such a search might have taken several weeks.

- Keep it short and sweet—E-mail works best when messages are short, almost brusque. The key is immediacy and responsiveness, not literary style. Beware: because it is so immediate, make sure you don't say anything you might regret later.

- Share the knowledge—give customers access to your company's E-mail system. It's a simple way to create bonds your competitors will find tough to challenge. Your customers can use E-mail to place orders, ask questions, and contact people at your company.

- Look ahead—two emerging technologies promise even greater benefits. Groupware (sometimes referred to as "E-mail on steroids") allows groups of even far-flung individuals to work together and share information. And wireless communications can free salespeople from phone lines, so you can send and receive information from notebook computers or personal digital assistants from remote locations without having to plug in.[2]

Why use E-mail?

E-mail can save time and money that is wasted by using the telephone and not getting through to the right party or waiting on hold. Initially replacing inter-office memos, now it has dozens of uses. Many employers consider it the most efficient vehicle to conduct certain types of business. Employees often consider it their private mail system. Until recently it was practical only for larger businesses for the simple reason that setting up and maintaining a computer network—which is necessary to support E-mail—was more trouble and expense than most small businesses could handle. Now E-mail has become a popular way for large companies, telecommuters, salespeople, and home office entrepreneurs to open new avenues of communication, solve problems, and network with other business professionals.

People who don't return phone calls often answer E-mail. Once a symbol of being a nerd, E-mail is now being used as a symbol of social empowerment and is a quickly growing means of communicating. E-mail is getting easier to use with point-and-click graphics.

A recent study at one medium-size firm estimated that it could save more than $100,000 a year in long-distance telephone costs if even 25 percent of its staff was hooked up to the Internet.

Cyber-service

If you're interested in on-line customer service which will provide your prospects and customers with information and assistance twenty-four hours a day, contact Communications Marketing and Distribution in Atlanta. Promotional materials, invoices, purchase orders, supplier updates, reports, and answers to questions can be sent by MCI Mail and its E-mail software, Microsoft Mail. When you sign up for the service and add your address, everything is handled like interoffice E-mail. And, best of all, it may save you money in the long run.

A list of Frequently Asked Questions and their answers is available in the Internet by sending an E-mail message to info@cdrom.com with the subject "FAQ."

The ticket's in the E-mail

"We're an E-mail company," says E.J. Hewitt, travel administration manager at Libbey-Owens-Ford Co. (LOF), a Toledo-based glassmaker. LOF uses Apollo Travel Service's system, offered by Thomas Cook Travel, whereby computers process travel requests, check flight options and fares, and return information to travelers within five minutes.[3]

Electronic conferencing

For a time and cost-effective way to conduct meetings, consider an electronic conferencing service called Convene. It combines E-mail, electronic bulletin boards, conference calls, and faxes into one service. With your personal computer, modem, and Convene software you can communicate with various departments within your organization, as well as your customers across town, in another state, or on the other side of the globe. You may start by talking one-to-one with your customer and expand the meeting as they need more information from one or more of their regional offices. You might need to include your inventory or shipping department, quality control, or the finance department in on the meeting.

Everyone can present needs, share information, gather ideas, and gain consensus without physically being together. Each participant can see all the comments and questions submitted by everyone else. A full text of all communications is automatically saved and can be printed at any time. Convene sees to it that all related messages are sent to and received from all participants. If you are working on a complicated sales agreement, everyone involved can submit their input and technical requirements and send the agreement back and forth until it is agreeable to everyone. Even if everyone involved in the meeting is traveling to different locations, you can still communicate with each other. If you are interested in this service, contact Convene International at 800 755-8995.

E-mail a telegram

Having trouble getting prospects to look at your sales message? Third-class mail is generally thrown away and priority mail doesn't have a much higher chance of getting to the buyer's desk. How about trying the old-fashioned telegram? An independent study revealed that 93 percent of those who get one can't resist opening and reading it. That's two times the rate of regular mail, including first class.[4]

John Stewart, cofounder of Audio Computer Information, sits in his farmhouse in the midst of cornfields in Spring Grove, Minnesota, and sends "telegrams" to media buyers. "Even if you're working out in the country on a single laptop," says Stewart, "you come off looking like a major corporation from downtown." Stewart uses DeskMail from Western Union Priority Services, types his messages on his PC and transmits them directly to Western Union where they format them and send them as telegrams. The software costs $30 and requires an IBM-type PC plus a modem. Each telegram sent by DeskMail costs $3.90 for overnight delivery or $1.59 for second-day delivery, compared to $15 for a conventional telegram.[5]

Forget prospecting by E-mail

Advertisers who send mass "junk-E-mail" can alienate potential clients who are charged "postage due." Frequently they respond by sending back "junk replies," which might be nonsense recipes or expressions of hostility.

E-mail advertising in any form is a major source of contention on the Net. James McBride, whose Los Altos–based marketing firm collected E-mail addresses by category and sold them to clients, has stopped selling them because of all the flak.

"People who don't like it will send you back hundreds of messages a day just for the hell of it, as an irritation," McBride says. "Everybody feels it's their job to police the Internet." McBride turned his address lists into the first analog cyberspace phone book. Published by IDG, the Internet White Pages is now available in stores.[6]

Use E-mail to get a jump on your competitors

When Helen Pastorino, president and partner in Alain Pinel Realtors in Northern California, saw an E-mail message that one of her rivals was closing down an office, she put her mind and computer to work. She E-mailed her 150 agents a message asking them to immediately start recruiting the soon-to-be displaced agents. Pastorino assumed the leasing of the closing Grubb & Ellis office under the condition that the tenants leave everything from phones to file cabinets. Then she E-mailed instructions for creating marketing materials and a press campaign. Less than a week after her rival announced it was closing its office and before many of its stunned officers had a chance to ask for equipment and recruit their out-of-work agents, Pastorino had her new office up and running.

"I don't know that you could move that fast without the technology," Pastorino states. She believes part of her speed and power come from her willingness to embrace computers, E-mail, and networking—which includes 367 networked workstations from Next Computer Co. Her firm offers its agents sophisticated, targeted advertising and far more technology than her competitors.

Pastorino's system includes a computer message board to enable management, clients, and partners to reach agents. Once agents log on to any machine in the firm's offices, operators, managers, and other agents know where they are. Calls are forwarded to other offices. If an agent is already on the line, the operator can let her know who's calling by flashing her E-mail.

Every agent in the company is automatically E-mailed about new properties. All listings are stored in the company-wide database which enables agents to search a listing by name, address, or ad copy and have the information in seconds. Jeff Barnett doubled his income and works less thanks to this technology. He spends a few minutes searching the MLS and prints out a market analysis on company stationery for his clients. He orders open house cards and prospecting letters by computer. He searches county records by modem, downloads the names and addresses, and prints out the cards. Without the computers it would have taken him two days to accomplish a task he now completes in minutes.

Barnett had a client who needed to sell a home in two days. After contacting fellow agents by E-mail, he got back a response from an agent who had an eager buyer. According to Barnett: "We tend to double end [represent both the buyer and seller] on more properties because of E-mail."

For $100 per month Pastorino expanded her E-mail to international access through Internet. "You can E-mail late at night when it's too late to call," says Pastorino. "People in Silicon Valley are used to a level of professionalism. It would be substandard if they had to wait two days for a realtor to return a call." Foreign and traveling clients stay in touch with their agents from as far away as Europe and Japan. Pastorino does partnering with companies that also use Nextware hardware and software. Every fifteen minutes Alain Pinel sends its title companies Internet mail on its latest closing properties so they don't have to play phone tag with escrow officers.

Jonathan Littman of *Forbes* magazine asked Pastorino if the same technology that enabled her firm to prosper in a down market might eventually render real estate firms obsolete, since computer bulletin boards already make listings and open house schedules available to PC users. To the contrary, Pastorino believes that real estate agents will continue to be valued as information resources who will facilitate the coordination of critical negotiations.[7]

Electronic mail or text communications systems may be integrated with voice mail on some systems. As technology advances in the area of changing voice from analog to digital so computers can understand it, we will see a wider range of options in this area. Some systems already integrate E-mail with voice mail, but in the future voices will be more readily changed to text and text to voice, with many applications including a voice activated fax machine.

More than E-mail

Notes is an E-mail program by Lotus with additional features allowing the sharing of documents, voice recordings, and even digitized video in a group, with everyone able to add new thoughts and review what has been said or produced before. Notes can be customized to fit various business needs. Its popularity created a niche in the software industry known as groupware.

Wireless E-mail

The office of today has no walls and no boundaries. To stay in touch, you need an E-mail system that goes where you go. ARDISmail is wireless messaging that enables you to maintain contact with your office E-mail system and with your coworkers when you're not in your office. There are no telephone jacks to search out and plug into. A laptop or palmtop computer with a radio modem is all the equipment you need to keep in touch— whether you're walking down the street, riding in a taxi, or stuck in an airport. ARDISmail is designed to work with your office E-mail system, not replace it. You can retrieve, leave, store, and forward messages from almost anywhere. You can communicate with customers and suppliers on systems other than your office E-mail, including most public E-mail systems and other wireless networks.

ARDISmail's automatic roaming capability keeps you in touch when you travel between customer locations, between cities, or across the country without incurring long-distance charges. Simply turn on your computer and you can instantly send or receive messages if you're in one of the 10,700 cities and towns across America they service.

E-mail out and video mail in?

Daniel R. Burk, president and founder of Compass Computer Services, Inc., a telecommunications consulting firm located in Falls Church, Virginia, predicts that by 2001, video mail will replace E-mail and voice mail. According to Burke, you will be able to pick up a handset, dial someone you want to talk to, and if that person is not available, leave a video message that person will be able to play back on her computer screen.[8] Think about the applications for selling. If an elusive client keeps evading that appointment, you leave a three-minute message on his video mail outlining the benefits and features of your new product or service. And after the sale is made, call him up on the computer and leave a one-minute message thanking him for the order and assuring him it was a wise decision.

To use or not to use

E-mail involves a certain amount of risk. Not only can E-mail messages be read by many people other than the intended recipients, but E-mail can be almost tracelessly forged—virtually no one receiving a message over the net can be sure it came from the ostensible sender.

One of the risks associated with a greater reliance on any technology is that it becomes increasingly impersonal. While E-mail has tremendous advantages that will render its increased use inevitable, it is also a tool that diminishes personality in the rapid transfer of memos, documents, etc. Regardless of how advanced our technology becomes, we will need to maintain personal touches and personal contact.[9] If you use E-mail to communicate with your clients, make sure it is the most appropriate vehicle for the situation and that you don't inadvertently press the wrong button and send confidential or embarrassing information to your customers.

Another problem is that an insidiously coded E-mail message can cause some computers to give the sender almost unlimited access to all the recipient's files. Mail-transfer programs are only one of many ways an attacker can gain access to a networked computer. "It's like the Wild West," says Donn B. Parker of SRI. "No laws, rapid growth and enterprise—it's shoot first or be killed."[10]

Private passwords may slow someone down if they are trying to gain access to your computer, but can frequently be guessed or located by others. Hackers are adept at breaking passwords, but new systems are being developed that scan the user's retina or fingerprint.

Hopefully E-mail will become more user-friendly in the coming years. AT&T's EasyLink division is working on offering a service that will convert text to voice and faxed documents to a text format that can be handled by a word processor. Along with it will come a single electronic mailbox instead of one for voice mail, E-mail, and fax mail. Received by your computer, it can include text, voice, fax, photographs, and video clips and be received by your pocket-sized or business card sized personal digital assistant, (PDA) or even a special wrist-watch like those you saw in Dick Tracy comics.[11]

Chapter 9

Dialing for $$$
(Telemarketing)

"On busy days in our telemarketing centers, I bring in buffet lunches, so people don't have to get up from their stations to go to lunch. But I haven't yet gotten them to accept the catheter idea I proposed."

—Jim McCann
CEO of 800-FLOWERS

Telephone technology is creating new ways to sell. Remote control phones, video phones, display phones, Scan Phones, compression units, predictive dialer software, Electronic Information Systems (EIS), Computer Telephone Integration (CTI), Uniform Call Distributors (UCD), Voice Response Units (VRU), Automated Response Units (ARU), Automated Call Distributors (ACD), telecomputers, personal communicators—don't look now, but your no-tech telephone is fast becoming a dinosaur. As you read about what others are doing, ask yourself how you can capitalize on the new telephone equipment and services to add a new dimension to your selling techniques.

Tele-personnel

Innovative businessman Tony Visone uses phone lines in a way even Alexander Graham Bell did not envision—to sustain a personless office!

Visone Corvette, the country's largest Corvette dealership, is about to open its sixth satellite showroom, which, like the others, will have no secretaries, no receptionists, and no bookkeepers. Visone's main office, in Saugus, Massachusetts, will perform functions for every other showroom by phone.

The enabling linkage is a fairly new technology that essentially compacts voice and electronic messages into digital "packets," which are inserted into gaps between the other messages on an already-paid-for data line. The packets are uncompacted at the other end. Micom Communications' relatively inexpensive ($3,000) Marathon Data/Voice Server makes it possible. One server unit is attached at each end of a 56,000-baud line leased from the phone company. The two units parcel the dedicated line into seven channels, permitting six voice conversations, plus a fax or computer data exchange, all at once. There are no long-distance charges.

Using conventional phone service, a company in Boston that communicates with its sales office in Chicago every day for two hours and sends another hour's worth of fax and computer traffic would spend about $8,400 per year in tolls (at 18 cents a minute). But it could lease a line for about $4,800, install two compression units for about $6,000, and come out well ahead after a few years of use.

Founder Tony Visone affirms, "I couldn't run the company without the compression units." Given the volume of phone and fax use Visone's near-$70-million company engages in every business day (twenty-five telemarketers work out of the Saugus office), the toaster-size apparatus has been a godsend. Monthly telecommunications costs now total about $4,000. Visone says that using the phones as much as he does now but without the compression units would cost him $70,000 per month.

Visone's operations in Atlanta, Indianapolis, Los Angeles, Peabody, Massachusetts, and Pompano, Florida funnel into the original Saugus site, where they're tied into a central local-area network. A dealer from any showroom can simply call the Saugus office, where archived documents can be called up on a computer, obviating the need for separate office staffs. Inventories, customers' needs, bills of sale, and similar information from each location are shared countrywide. "It's made the company one," Visone says.[1]

Sound unbelievable? Just wait. In a few years, you'll be examining sales orders or bids face to face with the person on the other end of a phone call. In some areas we can already answer ads that scroll across the display on screen-based phones. We have caller I.D. which tells us who's calling before we pick up the phone. And you can see the name of the person on call-waiting, and direct the call to voice mail if you don't want to answer.

Tele-advertising

Will consumers be willing to listen to a few words from their sponsor when they make a personal phone call? Seattle entrepreneur Harry Hart thinks so. He invented FreeFone Information Network because he believes putting advertisements on the telephone will be profitable for both consumers and advertisers.

Subscribers must answer a questionnaire providing demographic information about themselves, including age, lifestyle activities, income, and what they normally buy. Advertisers select only individuals in their target market, which could be as specific as their credit card holders who haven't used their credit card in the past month.

One Ford dealership in Seattle uses it to reach consumers who have recently placed a phone call to a competitor. Advertisers pay in accordance with how closely they want to pinpoint their subscriber base, ranging from $1.95 to $3.20 per subscriber, for ten messages per month.

Consumers punch in a personal code before making a phone call and are routed through FreeFone's computer which decides which message to play for them. Callers are paid approximately fifteen cents to listen to ads when they make phone calls. It might be as short as five seconds, saying "This phone call is sponsored by the Bon Marche department store," or considerably longer, depending on the options chosen.

If the individual wants more information she has several options which include pushing one button for further details, another button for a coupon, or another button to talk directly with the advertiser. Some subscribers especially like FreeFone's concert information and restaurant coupons.[2]

In Canada, New Brunswick Telephone is experimenting with Smart Talk, a service that enables companies to download advertising data to customers' homes. Participants come home, scroll through the selection of messages on the screen, and if they find one they want—say a two-for-one coupon from Domino's—they press a key and begin ordering.

Teleshopping

Not only can you make and receive phone calls on the plane, but you can also do your shopping while you fly. In-flight shopping on domestic flights generated $30 million in revenue in 1993. Phoenix-based SkyMall allows travelers to place their orders on the air phone and charge them to their credit cards. Travelers landing at Phoenix, Dallas/Ft. Worth, San Francisco, Los Angeles, Atlanta, Chicago, or Denver can have their purchases delivered to them at the airport gate if they order one hour before the flight lands. Catalogs are filled with convenience items and high-tech equipment ranging from laptop computers to fax machines, for the business travelers who realize they left something behind they need. Nearly half of SkyMall's customers are men. More than 30 percent are 35 to 44. The majority travel six to twenty-four times a year and have high incomes. Travelers also get frequent flier mileage for their purchases.[3]

Want to shop and pay bills without leaving home? You can pay your bills by using the "light pen" on the ScanFone, running it across a few bar codes on your personalized account, entering the date and the amount, and your bills are paid. ScanFone's built-in credit card reader, light pen, and display screen allow you to shop from catalogs without waiting to give them your credit card number and address. It's all in the phone.

For example, if you're interested in receiving a catalog from companies like Crate & Barrel, Crabtree & Evelyn, Barnes & Noble, Reliable Home Office, or Brookstone, you merely enter your passcode on your phone, press "2" for ordering, scan the "catalog code" and scan the bar code following each catalog description and you will receive the catalog in the mail.

When you want to order from the catalogs, use your light pen to scan the bar code of the item you want, then run your credit card through the reader on the phone. No more repeating your card number and address over the phone. No more talking to a telemarketer—just use your phone light pen and order.

ScanFone is not science fiction; it's being used throughout the United States for a minimal fee of $11.95 per month. If you use your phone to pay up to thirty bills per month, it saves you $9.60 on postage with a net cost to you of $2.35 per month.

Don't expect it to be faster than writing checks, however. You have to wait for ScanFone to make transactions and sometimes repeat them numerous times, but their customer service department excels in providing good service. PhonePlus, a new generation now being test-marketed, includes a built-in speaker phone, a personal directory, a larger screen, an alphabet keyboard, plus a built-in menu. ScanFone and PhonePlus are a preview of things to come; a great conversation piece; a novel way to impress your techno-laggard friends; and fun to use if you're not in a hurry.

Electronic classifieds

Dave Werling, senior manager for residential services and terminals at Northern Telecom, envisions that within the next couple of years electronic Yellow Pages and electronic classified ads will join such currently available services as pay-per-view TV and home banking.

Say you're looking for a used BMW. You tap into the local newspaper's classifieds, scroll through the car section, find one you're interested in, and press a soft key to be connected to the person who placed the ad. The phone network makes the connection so you don't know what number you dialed, saving you time and protecting the privacy of the seller.

Prodigy Services and the publishing arm of Nynex Corporation are developing Yellow Pages–style display advertising which will be delivered through the Prodigy online service. Advertisers will be able to update their ads every day, use colors, multiple screens, and interactive TV if consumers want more information. You can also just look up the phone number on your computer screen and eliminate the stack of Yellow Page directories associated with major metropolitan areas. Bell South Enterprises and Cox Enterprises Inc. are offering Yellow Pages and classified advertising through touch-tone telephones. The information will also be available on personal computers, fax machines, and other electronic devices.[4]

Let their fingers do the walking

GTE Yellow Pages offers a Quick Tips service whereby interested customers can call a number found near your listing in the Yellow Pages and hear a recording regarding how to select a specific type of business or service. At the end of the information the recording will say, "This Quick Tip is brought to you by . . ."

If you press * or 1 you will be connected directly with the business. This service allows you to reach your highly motivated buyers who are looking in the Yellow Pages trying to decide who to call. An advertiser sponsoring consumer advice lends credibility to the advertiser. For more information call GTE at 214 453-7135.

Phone a home and all the trimmings

Thinking of moving to Arizona? *Home Buying Choices* magazine offers a program through the *Arizona Republic* and *Phoenix Gazette* to request information about specific properties or search for homes that fit your general specifications. All you need is a touch-tone phone. Automated searches are completed by computer and the results are read to you. Call 602 271-5656 and press 1000 to reach the Homes By Phone service. Then select option 2 and follow the voice instruction.

Need an apartment? Rent Line in Reseda, California offers a twenty-four-hour phone service to help you look for an apartment. Landlords pay $149 per month.

Once you find that home or apartment you might not want to pass out on the floor. Dial-a-Mattress will deliver a mattress to you within two hours of the sale if you live in one of the major cities where they do business. And while you're waiting, you can "dial-a-beer" by calling 800 761-BEER for the U.S. Beer Club or 800 854-BEER for Beer Across America.

Automobiles by phone

The Vehicle Information Network in Westlake, California will fax car shoppers a qualified list of used cars and trucks at no charge. A one-time fee of $14.95 is charged to list a car or truck until it sells. Dealers pay $795 for unlimited number of lists. Dial 800 CAR-SEARCH.

Telemarketing

Lens Express of Fort Lauderdale, Florida wanted to expand its telemarketing operations, but was having a hard time keeping telemarketers. To help its phone solicitors reach prospects quickly and earn more, the company bought predictive dialer software. "It dials through the customer database very rapidly and detects those that don't answer, disconnected numbers, busy signals, and even answering machines, and delivers to the sales agent a live person," according to Brian O'Neill, president of Lens Express.

Orders are taken on-screen and delivered electronically to the stockroom. An order is processed with a single slip of paper printed there; the paper has a tear-off label for shipping. The rest is kept for billing and records. The cost is not great. The charge for software varies according to the company's size. Phone calls run a penny each.

According to O'Neill, "The next thing we'll look at is having sales agents work at home." Not too far in the future, an employee will be able to be anywhere, with the dialing software routing calls automatically to the next available phone solicitor, wherever he or she is.[5]

According to industry estimates, 70 percent of all business today is conducted by telephone. More than five hundred thousand companies are currently using "800" numbers, an increase of 7 percent between 1992 and 1993. To manage this critical activity, thousands of organizations have established telephone call centers. Many of them, like Lens Express, have turned to Electronic Information Systems (EIS), the world's leading provider of outbound computer-telephone integration (CTI) technology.

How does CTI work?

EIS systems dial long lists of telephone numbers and switches only those telephone calls answered by an individual. The systems filter out busy signals, ringing phones, and recorded telephone messages. This results in a large number of connections in a short period of time. Statistically, dials that don't connect take 65 to 75 percent of a caller's time. Productivity, as measured by the amount of time agents speak to respondents (talk time), can increase by 100 to 200 percent.

As soon as a connection is made, detailed demographic and biographical information about the called party flashes on the agent's computer screen, as well as the script. This information—purchasing history, age, address, etc.—is used by the telephone agent to help the transaction proceed efficiently and smoothly.

The system predicts how many dials to make to keep callers busy without hanging up on prospects. It continuously adjusts the dialing rate as the calling conditions change—such as caller availability, percentage of completed dials, and average call length. Preview dialing lets callers see the record before the call is placed. Inbound campaigns distribute incoming calls to a group of agents who are trained to handle customer and prospect questions. The system automatically redials no-answers and busies at specified intervals and can be set to identify answering machines automatically and reschedule those calls as well. The result: more efficient calling and higher penetration of calling lists.

By linking the telephone with the computer, EIS systems have given customers triple-digit productivity gains, increased agent effectiveness and total management of the call center environment. As these trends continue, inbound centers handling "800" number calls for consumer products, catalogs, infomercials, and home shopping services present vast new opportunities as they integrate outbound calling into their operations.

But what about the little guy?

If your company isn't ready to invest in CTI technology, look into some of the software for telemarketers. TeleMagic for DOS sells for $499 and offers telemarketing scripts, call logging and timing, as well as dozens of other features, including networking, to support telephone sales work. TeleMagic for Windows also sells for $499 but offers a three-level click of a button approach to contacts—company data, contact data, and associated data. For more information call 800 835-MAGIC, but make sure your computer has enough memory to install these programs.

Call Interactive in Omaha, Nebraska offers a wide variety of telemarketing, prospecting, promotion, and customer service programs that can make a one-person business appear to be a major corporation open twenty-four hours a day. Their fax number is 402 498-7900.

High IQ phones

The applications for new phone technology are almost limitless. "What's going on in the telephone industry," says Larry Moore, president of Philips Home Services, "is that networks are becoming more intelligent and are able to deliver services that would have been unheard of in science fiction ten years ago."[6]

Home-office workers in particular should benefit big time from the interactive phones. Moore's crystal ball portends, among other things, a national phone directory accessible by screen and Auto Number ID, a billing-assist feature that stores the numbers you've called over a period of time and shows who was called and how long you spoke.

For $639, the Philips P100 phone—part PC, part phone—adds a keyboard, which can be used as a Telecommunications Device for the Deaf (TDD), a 5-inch text display of 16 lines, a 2400-band modem, a parallel printer output, and a smart-card reader. In the future, smart cards could contain information including personal identification and credit card numbers so you don't have to key in that same information every time you purchase an airline ticket or an item from a catalog via an automated system.

Screen-based phones

As products and services begin to roll out, you'll start to hear a lot about screen-based phones. Many of the services and capabilities screen-based phones offer are already available via personal computers and other means. However, telephone equipment and service companies are banking on the assumption people want these interactive services to be more easily accessible.

What better way, the telecommunications industry puts forth, than with the telephone? Over 90 percent of U.S. households have a phone, with a user interface even technophobes are comfortable with. Only 30 percent of U.S. homes have a computer.

The screen-based or display phone will change the way you do business. According to Moore, the transition to screen-based phones is as revolutionary as the conversion from rotary to touch-tone phones. The phone and service options are available on a significant basis. Jupiter Communications, a market research group, predicts 17 million households will have screen-based phones by 1997; by the turn of the millennium, the number will be 33 million. Five years from now, Moore says, "people are going to say, 'I can't believe we ever lived without them.'"[7]

While the transition to screen-based phones will make many services easier to access, display phones will also get people accustomed to *looking at* their telephones.

By the turn of the century, industry sources say, we'll be straightening ties and combing hair before we "dial" the phone. Analog videophones are available now, but their quality isn't acceptable for serious use. They lack full-duplex audio, which means one person has to finish before the other can speak and be heard; they also lack full-motion video so movements appear jerky and in slow motion.

MCI offers a VideoPhone which transmits ten frames per second, works internationally and sends/receives full-color images over standard analog phone lines. With this phone you can show your product to your clients rather than just explaining it. Add the speaker function and use it for conference calls. Available for $899 through the Sharper Image Catalog at 800 344-4444.

When it's a reality, visual communications will mean a lot more than just seeing a face on the other end of the line. "The videophone technology will improve," says Mike Zeaman, district manager for public relations of AT&T Consumer Products, "and as time goes by it will be lower in cost. We see visual communications being a part of people's everyday lives." He cites interactive applications such as playing video games against others over the phone, and accessing information services.

"It will be like a library that never closes," Zeaman says. "Rather than going to a shelf to pick up a book, you'll be going to your screen to access documents, photos or diagrams."

Is that a telephone screen, a computer screen, or a TV screen? No one's sure. "We're talking about interactive voice, data and visual communication all at once," Zeaman says. "You won't have to have a separate computer, game device, and telephone. The whole breadth is going to come together, and all those things are going to happen with one device. Whoever does it best is going to be the winner."

And that means a lot of companies with their fingers in different pots. AT&T will use its telecommunications and computer expertise; companies like Sony will use their video monitor and audio/video expertise.

"We started with the lowest quality form of video telecommunications," says Leo Flotron, marketing manager for video conferencing at Sony, regarding the industry's current generation of videophones. "But there are lots of people working on computer-based video-teleconferencing products that could potentially be of much higher quality."[8]

Intel Architecture Lab (IAL) created ProShare, a software that allows two PC users connected by a telephone line to work together onscreen. With ProShare, either PC can "host" the other, so the users see exactly the same data and share the same program. If the phone line linking the machines is a high-speed integrated services digital network (ISDN) line, ProShare also lets the users conduct a video conference as they work, with the help of miniature cameras mounted on the PCs.

Also, in collaboration with Microsoft, IAL defined standards that allow a PC equipped with a speaker and microphone to double as a programmable telephone. Intel is developing software that will endow Pentium computers with the power to handle telephone functions. Soon you'll be able to connect a phone line to the back of your PC and have it set up your conference calls.

"What I'm after is televisions and telephones and every single-purpose appliance," says Intel's CEO Andy Grove. "The best way for us to go for the 250 million-unit market is to move video telephony and conferencing and entertainment and information access onto the PC and render those other things less and less relevant."[9]

Tapping the phone lines

Welcome to the information revolution. You'll have more facts, figures, and fun and games at your fingertips than you ever thought possible—maybe more than you'd ever want. And this new technology will have many ramifications for your sales career. Will your product or service be sold on a phone shopping network or will you be doing your own telemarketing on the videophones?

If you think telephone technology doesn't present new opportunities for selling your product or service, think about William Orton, president of Western Union. Due to his limited imagination and lack of vision, in 1876 Orton turned down exclusive rights to the telephone for $100,000 with the statement, "What use could this company make of an electrical toy?"

You don't have to become a phonophile, but your competitors will be using the latest "electrical toy" and you'll be subjected to a wide array of new services and technology.

Information overload? You can always hang up the phone.

Chapter 10

Welcome to Voice Mail Jail

"Among the more frustrating technology developments of recent years are the automated phone-answering systems that imprison callers in loops, sentencing them to listen to endless recorded messages. Potential customers are left yearning for a human voice or just to go back to the previous menu."

—*Inc.* magazine

Why do we have to put up with it?

Although it's a form of electronic conversation we love to hate, the voice mail industry just keeps growing and growing and growing, over 40 percent each year from 1987 to 1991. Against the goodwill and wishes of their customers, three-quarters of the Fortune 2000 companies use voice mail.

According to the North American Telecommunications Association, there were more than 2 million subscribers to voice mail systems in 1993 and there will be 14.7 million subscribers by 1995. In 1992, the market for voice/call processing equipment topped $2.9 billion and is still growing.

Eighty-nine percent of mailbox owners considered voice mail essential to their business, and 78 percent said voice mail improved their job productivity. For the users, however, it's a different story. In a survey conducted by *Inc.* magazine, 12 percent of respondents described it as "loathsome." Sixteen percent felt it was indispensable, 24 percent felt it was worthwhile, and 28 percent felt they could live with it. Twenty-one percent do not use it.[1]

The authors of *The Virtual Corporation* confirm that "our lives will increasingly be dominated by machines that perform tasks for us. In many cases this will be a less personal world; the first clues can be experienced now whenever we deal with an ATM rather than a human teller, or when our phone calls are answered by a voice mail machine."[2]

TechnoTrends author Daniel Burrus believes we will soon be using visual voice-mail on a telecomputer, which is a "combination of a Touch-Tone telephone, answering machine, fax, and home computer with a flat-panel display using an electronic pen or touch screen for making selections or imputing information . . . Multimedia voice-mailboxes will be another popular option."[3]

Like it or not, techno-selling includes voice messaging and it's here to stay, so we may as well find the best ways to use it and avoid the destructive ones.

What will it do for you?

In addition to basic phone answering and routing functions, voice mail can tell you when a message was delivered and by whom, save messages and place them in different queues, forward messages to other mailboxes with introductory comments, and notify the recipient at another number that a message has been received.

Other functions include giving recorded information back to callers and sending the information by fax to callers who request the information. If your fax and voice mail are interfaced, when you receive a fax or a voice mail message it will notify you on your cellular phone, beeper, or another number. You can then instruct your voice mail where to send the fax—to your hotel in the Caribbean or your printer at home.

Your electronic mail or text communications system may be integrated with your voice mail on some systems. As technology advances in the area of changing voice from analog to digital so computers can understand it, we will see a wider range of options in this area. Some systems already integrate E-mail with voice mail but in the future, voices will be more readily changed to text and text to voice, with many applications—including a voice activated fax machine.

Advantages of voice mail

Voice mail is efficient in that one piece of equipment will handle the private message needs of numerous individuals anytime or anyplace. Within the company, messages can be sent to or received by several people in several different departments at one time. Messages can be forwarded to other mailboxes with preface remarks. Voice mail provides a high degree of accuracy in tone and nuance as well as information.

Each individual is provided with a voice "mailbox" which is basically a data file on a computer. With a Touch-Tone phone the user can access or erase selected messages or change the outgoing message.

If used properly, many more incoming calls and messages can be handled at one time, saving the expense of operators and lost calls.

For people dealing in international business, voice mail can be especially valuable in dealing with time differences.

Callers can review their message and change it if they said something they regret or wasn't clear, or prioritize messages so theirs is first.

Guest mailboxes are available for those who don't have voice mail but for whom you want to leave a message on your system.

Voice mail eliminates phone tag—if you need to get a message to someone but it isn't necessary to talk to them or their line is busy, voice mail will do it for you. It keeps you in front of your customers by staying in touch on your terms. Let your clients know you're thinking of them by leaving a short message over the weekend so they have it first thing when they get in on Monday.

Disadvantages of voice mail

Voice-messaging technology has earned a bad reputation among many users. Some companies have badly misused their systems and bypassed the personal touch, as well as using the system to screen calls and avoid bill collectors and unwanted or unprofessional salespeople.

Most callers hate electronic greetings when they call a business. It's the impersonality of the voice-processing systems that is aggravating, especially the ones that present a multilevel menu of options. They hate listening to interminable lists of numbers they can't remember while trying to figure out whether to press stars or pounds—only to find out that while they were dinking around on the phone pad, a long awaited return call has come in. And that the caller has left a long, meandering message that swallowed his phone number.

Customers feel they are being given the runaround and get frustrated when they punch button after button and end up right back at the original message even though they obeyed all the instructions. Frequently callers spend more time trying to get to the department they need to talk to than they do transacting their business.

Voice mail doesn't represent the highest form of customer service and gives the appearance that the company is actually avoiding the customer. Companies realize the financial benefits, but callers pay the price in time and aggravation. Whereas customers used to say, "The check is in the mail," now they screen the calls, don't answer, and don't return calls.

The aggravation to the customer or client feeling trapped in the voice mail calling system can be costly in good customer relations and goodwill. When a customer needs that human touch and continues to get kicked around the voice mail system, he may give in to an emotional outburst and swear never to try again.

Improperly used, voice mail can be costly in goodwill and customer relations. Business consultant Cliff Eggink of Scottsdale concurs and states, "I don't think any voice mail system is going to make an unhappy customer happy." Most people he deals with consider it a "necessary evil."[4]

Should you use voice mail?

Voice mail is "one of the most destructive tools of the '90s because companies use it to avoid talking to customers," says

John Tschohl, head of the Service Quality Institute in Minneapolis, and author of *Achieving Excellence Through Customer Service* and *The Customer is Boss*. "The vast majority of people hate it. If you have too many customers and too much business, then it's a great system to install. If you want to improve sales, rip it out within 24 hours."[5]

David Ladd, who is credited with being voice mail's inventor, says it's not his fault that sales professionals have had to learn to leap enormous voice-mail hurdles. The technology was meant for internal use only, as in "Great job, Max. Your $10,000 raise takes effect on Monday. Just wanted you to have a nice weekend."[6]

Why use voice mail? Various surveys have shown that three-fourths of all calls are not completed on the first attempt because the person is out or on the line. Over 50 percent of all phone calls are placed to convey information in one direction and do not require a response. An AT&T survey revealed that two-thirds of all calls were considered less important than the work they interrupted. Often, therefore, just leaving a message is sufficient.

Using voice mail more effectively

There are several schools of thought on voice mail. Many believe it should be used on all incoming calls and throughout the company. Some believe it should be reserved for internal use only. Those who believe technology is changing the way we sell will find creative ways to use it to their advantage.

If you have so much business you find it necessary to use voice mail, include an option for the customer to talk to a real live person during business hours rather than going through a maze of recordings. Some people believe that if you want to increase your sales and efficiency, don't use it with your customers, use it internally. Opponents of voice mail say if cutting costs is a higher priority than increasing sales volume, go ahead and use it, but use it carefully.

Some customers don't mind using voice mail—studies report that over 50 percent of callers are not offended by it. A growing number of companies, however, are simply hanging up their call-processing equipment for outside callers and using it internally only.

In *The One to One Future*, Peppers and Rogers recommend a voice mail customer service which assigns a temporary voice mail number to the customer so they can call back and get their answer from your voice mail system. They suggested a message similar to the following: "Thank you for calling our customer service line. We cannot answer your call right now, but if you leave a message at the tone, we will have an answer for you in 24 hours. You can retrieve your answer by calling back and accessing our voice-mail system. Your personal, temporary, voice mailbox is pound 2322. If you would prefer us to call you back, be sure to tell us your phone number and suggest a convenient time to call."[7]

American Express uses prerecorded voice messages for their Privileges on Call (POC) service. Members call an "800" number, punch in their card number, and then listen to several choices until they find the one they want. If you're going to Memphis and need suggestions on which hotels and restaurants to patronize, you will not only be given the recorded information, but will receive special discounts if you use your American Express Card.

Guidelines for using voice mail

- If you use voice mail, find creative ways to implement it. Don't just use it as a receptionist.
- Make it interactive with your fax machine so customers can order merchandise, brochures, or price sheets.
- Let people know when they will be able to reach you and have a call forwarding option so whenever possible you will receive calls wherever you are.
- Provide the option of directly transferring the call to a person in customer service, inventory, billing, or another department they might need.
- Leave a simple, brief message and change it often. Don't offer too many options—no more than four at once.
- Check often for return messages and make sure your mail box doesn't fill up.
- Return your calls promptly, at least every three hours.

When you call someone else's voice mail

- Make a statement—call from a golf course and say "Wish you were here" or "Let's set up a date to play."

- Speak slowly and repeat your number—a common complaint is people leaving messages and numbers that aren't audible. Make sure your voice isn't offensive or doesn't set off the system by sounding like one of the numbers on a Touch-Tone phone. A high-pitched voice could mimic the pound sign, trigger the system, and send your call off into hyperspace—or somebody else's mailbox.

- Learn how to get to a real person even if you aren't given that option—for some systems all your need to do is hit the pound key and for others hit the zero key. Find out the secretary's extension and write it down. When you call back you might be able to bypass the menu by punching in the secretary's extension.

- If all else fails, fax or call back.

Make sure your system is secure

We don't even like to think about it, but there are many instances in which competitors bidding on the same job have acted on inside information which was later traced to picking up the information from someone else's voice mail. Be very careful about what kind of information you ask people to leave on your voice mail.

Don't leave confidential information on someone else's voice mail. Don't leave your bid figures for a job or other information that a competitor might like to know. It is possible to electronically break into some voice mail systems; some sales contracts are large enough to provide the incentive for unscrupulous salespeople to try to obtain information any way they can.

Hotel voice mail systems are notoriously easy to crack. A voice mail crook can generally access your voice mail by using your room number. Even if someone isn't trying to access your mail it can happen accidentally. According to *Forbes* magazine, Michael Stedman wanted to interview Robert Gates, the former director of the CIA. He phoned the Inn at Harvard in Cambridge, where Gates was staying, and was given a room number. When he called that number, he heard all Gates' voice messages being played back.[8]

How much does it cost?

Small companies can purchase a voice mail system for as little as $1,000. Medium companies might spend a few thousand dollars and large companies will probably spend over $100,000. Like all electronics, however, a system that once cost over $275,000 now costs as little as $8,000. But, you don't have to own your own equipment. Many companies offer a service bureau to which you can subscribe.

If you are considering purchasing a voice messaging system, a good analysis of the alternatives is available in *What to Buy for Business*, an independent consumer guide to business equipment and services. It offers a special edition on voice messaging. Some companies to contact about packages offering voice mail, fax services, call accounting, and phone-system administration are:

AT&T (800 247-7000)

Integrated Solution III

Merlin Legend

Definity Communications System

Partner Mail

PassageWay

Northern Telecom (800 NORTHERN)

Norstar

Startalk

Access Toolkit

And if you want to make your portable phones link into your office network, ask about Southwestern Bell Mobile System's FreedomLink (314 984-2379).

Chapter 11

Fax to the Max

"Savvy business owners are finding hundreds of new uses for fax response technology."

—Tom Kadala, President & Founder
Alternative Technology Corporation

To close the buyer-seller loop, state-of-the-art fax technology can be used to relay information in a matter of minutes to prospects who request it through an interactive, voice prompted phone system. All your brochures, advertisements, and other forms of customer communication can include a special number customers can call to access the service. You can change your information as often as you want and get information on who called and what they requested.

With this system, when clients ask for more information on your products, you answer, "Give me a fax number and you'll have it right now." Or, you can give your client the fax number and let him call in and choose which information he wants and who it should go to. When called, the system lists the information available. For example, the menu can say, "Extension 101 is a product price list. Extension 102 has information on our financing plan. Extension 103 is the specifications on our deluxe model." The customer selects the information and puts in his own fax number and hangs up. The information is immediately sent to the fax machine he requested.

If you want to see how easy it is to use, put this book down right now and call 914 478-5906 or 800 763-SEND. Punch in Extension 726. The machine will ask for your fax number and extension. After you punch it in, information on MarketFax will immediately be faxed to you.

MarketFax is a new technology from Alternative Technology Corporation in Hastings-on-Hudson, New York, which allows you to increase your sales force without hiring more staff. It combines new computer technology with voice cards, fax boards, and easy to use software to create a whole new type of information system. It's a better way to deliver information. It responds to clients instantaneously when they are interested and gives them exactly what you want them to see. This entirely new service can be put to work for you. It's easy for your clients to use, and changes how you get information into the hands of people who want it. The system stores codes for up to one thousand separate multipage documents, graphics, or photos. No typing or data input is involved—all you need to do is scan your literature into the system.

The MarketFax system is a complete package including a personal computer with a scanner, some specialized computer boards, and amazing software. All you do is plug it in, scan in your documents and begin telling people how to get it. Market-Fax has enough extra capacity that you can lease extra extensions to associates to help defray costs. It will monitor each account and automatically fax monthly statements. You can connect it to a "900" phone line and sell information on your own or other people's products.

Here are some examples of how fax technology is being used.

Faxed facts fast

The Boston Computer Exchange took all the documents they normally mailed to their clients and put them into the MarketFax system. They have price sheets, news items, hot products, policy statements, listing forms, nine-year price comparisons, order forms, and everything else. It's all available to any client anywhere in the world who has a fax machine. All they do is make the call, select what they want, and it's faxed right to the requesting party.

Americas Trading Company in New York uses MarketFax to list auctions and inventory liquidations. Everything they have in writing is available to all clients, anytime, to any fax machine.

Advertisers on 1010 WINS radio use a special WINS-FAX "800" number plus their own three-digit ID code number. This number is mentioned in the advertiser's commercial or in the 1010 WINS WINS-FAX special promo. Interested listeners use the phone to call the "800" number and punch in the advertisers' special code. Within sixty seconds, the information is received by the 1010 WINS listener.

Radio station WHTZ in New York uses MarketFax as a conference call mechanism. Before they started using MarketFax, each week the sales manager had a conference call with the national sales people in the rep firms, at a cost of about $500 each month, so he could give them the updated figures.

With MarketFax technology, the manager of the station updates the numbers on the Arbitron ratings each week and stores the information in the fax. The salespeople call in once a week, punch in their PIN numbers, and retrieve new rating numbers. Once they have this information, they can create new charts and graphics on their Tap Scan software with up-to-the-minute cost-per-thousand numbers. They can then make a presentation with their immediate ratings (which, hopefully, will be higher), and the rep can sell time for increased rates.

The presentation is made to an advertiser before the new Arbitron ratings are received in the mail showing them WHTZ's new ratings. If they have improved 2 percent it might increase their rates from $400 to $600 during morning drive time. If a client is trying to decide between several different stations, she's going to be impressed by the professionalism of the salesperson who can bring her updated ratings on colored graphics before the client receives the information in the mail.

This system also allows WHTZ to monitor the frequency of the salespeople's calls and what time periods they requested ratings for. It also shows when they called and just how anxious they are to obtain the updated figures which will help them in their presentations.

Seafax, a Portland, Maine credit information clearinghouse for the food industry, sends out four hundred identical newsletters every morning. If Seafax sent them out, it would take three hours' time on dedicated fax lines, or a major investment in new equipment and phone lines. Instead they use Xpedite and it only takes about three minutes if the receiver's lines are open. An advantage is that their machines keep dialing until they connect. In time-is-of-the-essence documents, the direct PC-to-broadcaster interface or "blast-a-fax" technology saves time and money, plus it allows the customer a jump on the competitor.

The Hats Off restaurant, in Hudson, Massachusetts, uses WinFax Pro to fax out menus describing the restaurant's specials at a specified time every night. The menus are updated during the day and faxed to all customers on a list, along with the restaurant's customized cover sheet.

"It's a great advertising tool," says owner Jim Griffin. "Customers get to work in the morning, and there's a fax waiting with our lunch specials on it. It tends to whet your appetite. The first month we used WinFax Pro, we saw tremendous growth in business—on the order of 40 to 50 percent."[1]

Just as important, the fax/modem has cut down on the workload at Hats Off restaurant. "The faxes virtually eliminated the problem of excess work," says Griffin. "We've even cut a hostess position, thanks to fewer phone calls."[2]

Fax technology may be old hat by now, but new players and new capabilities have made it more valuable than ever.

One-to-one marketing

Fax response technology creates your demographic base for you. For example, if you advertise in a certain magazine with a circulation of five hundred thousand you might assume that maybe five thousand of the readers are your potential customers. By putting your "800" number in the ad, only those customers who are interested in your products will call the number and request further information. Maybe you advertise the same or different products or services in different magazines. The Marketfax database will collect that information for you and tell you which customers responded to which ads on what days, how many different ads they responded to, and which products they are interested in.

Several periodicals use fax bulletin boards for reader service card information.

Newsweek magazine uses MarketFax for some of their advertisers. If you want more information about some of their travel advertisers, call 800 447 WEEK, punch in the advertiser code, and it's yours.

Golf Digest offers Golf Fax and *Golf* magazine offers Tee-Fax Service. Readers who want to find out more about a resort or package they read about in the ad dial an "800" number and press the three-digit number for the topics they want to learn more about. Within minutes they receive a complete package of information on their fax machine. The advertisers also obtain complete information on who is inquiring about their services and from which magazines.

Home Office Computing will fax a copy of any article in their magazine for a small fee. Call their "800" number, punch in the codes for the articles you want plus your credit card information, and the articles will be faxed to you instantly.

Want to take a fantasy cruise? *Travel Agent* magazine offers a variety of detailed information on cruises and cruise lines. Their ads give complete instructions to their readers. Call 800 227-5638 and request Ext. 275 and you will receive information about fantasy cruises.

Lawyer's Weekly sells daily fax summaries of selected federal, state, and local court opinions. MacWarehouse, for Macintosh users, uses a fax bulletin board for their catalog. Standard and Poor's will fax credit reports to regular customers of its credit bureau.

For $12 a month the *Los Angeles Times* offers Financial Fax, whereby you can follow fifteen stocks on a daily basis. Each day you will be faxed a summary of the volume, high, low, closing price, and net changes, along with key market index figures. If you're not going to be at your regular location, notify the fax machine where to send your faxes and for what length of time.

If you're reading *Wine Spectator* magazine and feel like dining out in a restaurant that allows you to enjoy a good cigar with your meal, dial 800 227-5638 Ext. 395 and you will receive a list of cigar-friendly restaurants close to you.

The *Wall Street Journal* offers tomorrow's headlines today with JournalFax, a newsletter delivered every business day to your fax machine. Two pages of business and financial news highlights and key closing market statistics drawn from the worldwide reporting of Dow Jones News Services are available to subscribers. Call 800 759-9966 for a sample copy.

The *WSJ* also offers Customclips to save you searching, sorting, and clipping time. They will scan the Dow Jones newswires and monitor your clients, prospects, and competitors, anticipate hot industry developments, analyze advertising, sales, and marketing strategies, and deliver the information to your fax or E-mail. For a monthly fee of $15 plus $3 per page for custom news you can be a step ahead of your competitors. Call 800 445-9454, Ext. 911.

If tax deadline is near and you haven't bothered to order those specialized tax forms you need, call The Wall Street Journal Tax Form Faxline at 800 414-4567 and they will deliver personal or corporate income tax forms to your fax machine twenty-four hours a day, seven days a week for $5 each.

Telemarketing applications

Your telemarketing department will love the solid leads which come in on the fax. Every person who calls in response to a fax number or an ad is a potential buyer. Eighty percent of those who respond leave their phone number. When telemarketers call the customer they have their entire calling record. They know where the prospects live, which products they are interested in, how many times they responded to different ads, what magazines they read, and what time of day they read them. MarketFax eliminates the need for cold calls. Instead, telemarketers will have an unbiased list of callers who called at will.

Homes by Fax

The Arizona Regional Multiple Listing Service offers *Home Buying Choices* as a free service through local newspapers, the *Arizona Republic* and the *Phoenix Gazette*. Prospective home buyers find a home that interests them in *Home Buying Choices*, a real estate magazine available at local supermarkets or convenience stores. All properties in the magazine are identified by an access code. By using the code to request information, a free flier is transmitted in minutes by fax machine. If you don't have a particular property in mind, but know, for example, you want a home with a swimming pool and a corral for your Arabians, it will fax you information about homes offering those amenities.

According to real estate agent Dean Selvey, "The fax machine has caused the biggest change in our industry. Contracts, escrows and closing papers are easily transmitted by fax machine, which results in speeding up real estate transactions. In the past, before faxes, transactions could take days or weeks. Now, we might complete an entire transaction without even seeing the seller."[3]

Why fax it to 'em?

By using a fax machine it takes less time to do business by speeding up the usual time required to generate and respond to time-sensitive documents. Send your customers a sales proposal or contract by fax for approval or verification, and once an agreement is reached, send a hard copy by mail. Fax machines are cost-effective and will pay for themselves in a very short period of time, eliminating much of the need for expensive next-day mail service.

Send thank-you notes by fax or appointment reminders. After you talk to a client or prospective client on the phone, follow up the call with an immediate fax thanking them for their time and summing up the points discussed. Or fax information prior to an appointment. If you are on top of the situation before the sale, the prospect will assume you will also follow through after the sale.

How to Pick a Provider

Consider in-house equipment. Call MarketFax at 914 478-5900. Tom Kadala, founder and president of Alternative Technology Corporation, will be happy to work with you to find creative applications for your business and help you determine whether or not it is economically feasible to own your own equipment.

147

Shop Around. Fax broadcasting is an efficient, cost-effective way to reach hundreds, even thousands, of customers with one stroke. It is more convenient than sending faxes one by one. And, when compared with bulk mailings, it saves time and significant dollars. With the proliferation of providers and services, it's wise to shop around. Here are some things to look for.

Inspect the package. When the broadcast fax service is priced as a package—that is, with all of the features and long-distance charges bundled together—be sure to analyze it carefully to determine exactly what portion of the price is for service and what portion goes to long-distance charges.

Report in. Make sure the fax reports give you all the information you need to manage your broadcast program. Among the items included should be the time the fax was delivered, how long it took, the number of attempts made, the lists used, names of persons to whom it was addressed, and summaries of total faxes delivered and not delivered.

Go the distance. If you are using one of the Baby Bells or a service company, check that it uses more than one long-distance phone carrier. That way, your faxes will not be held up in the event one carrier has transmission problems.

See a specialist. Some of the providers, especially the service companies, have "marketing specialists" who can help you identify new markets and new ways of using fax services. With their input, you can maximize the benefits of broadcast fax technology to meet your own specific needs.

Size up storage. Make sure your service provider has the list storage capability you need—both now and in the future. The same holds for graphics storage: even if you don't need it now, you may want to include that capability down the road.

See into the future. Ask what plans your provider has for the future. Fax technology will continue to evolve, leading to new, more sophisticated applications such as desktop capabilities and other customer-service applications. Make sure your provider is on top of the latest developments.[4]

Ancillary equipment and supplies

Whether or not you have a need for fax-on-demand technology, here are some products that will make your fax machine more productive for you:

Combine your fax and answering machine

If you've ever sat around the office waiting for a fax to come in, you will appreciate the new fax/digital answering machine from Brother. The Brother IntelliFAX 780 Message Center is more than an ordinary fax machine. It's more like a private assistant, forwarding and retrieving voice and fax messages, freeing you to schedule your day more productively.

Easily programmed, this model enables you to stay in touch with clients even while you're out on the road. You can access fax and phone messages whether you're at your hotel in L.A., your main office in South Carolina, your apartment in the city, or your weekend retreat at the shore. You can access important information anywhere at all.

The IntelliFAX 780 Message Center has a fifty page memory for storing faxes, out of paper reception, and broadcasting. The built-in digital answering machine provides up to twelve minutes of recording, quick access (play/erase/skip/repeat), remote access with ID code, and selectable message length. It can even forward your faxes to another fax or notify your personal pager if messages have been received.

Three-in-one

National Semiconductor makes TyIn 2000, which combines a telephone answering machine, send-and-receive fax machine, and a normal data modem for under $300. It will send faxes, data, and recorded voice messages and separate those functions into personal mailboxes. Salespeople or customers can call in, use their code, and either leave or receive messages for that coded mailbox. For more information call 408 721-4210.

Travel fax

If you don't want to carry a portable printer with you when you travel, you can use a phone jack and the fax-modem board inside your computer to send the information to the nearest fax machine. For example, fax the document to yourself at your hotel. All right, if you're a camper and the National Park doesn't have a fax machine, expect to spend between $900 and $1900, and look into the portable units offered by calling 800 FORA-FAX and 800 STAR-FAX. Their battery-powered units will allow you to do your faxing from the closest phone booth.

Xerox's Paperworks (800 4FAX-FAX) allows you to issue commands to your office or home PC while on the road. For example, if you're in a hotel and want to check your home or office faxes, use this software to notify your home computer. In a few minutes you will receive a list of all the faxes received since you last checked. If you want to see a few of them but not all, check them off and fax it back. The home or office machine will send the faxes you want to whatever location you specify. And if you forget the forms you need, not to worry. Notify your machine by phone to fax the correct forms.

Fax Line Manager(tm)

Instead of installing additional phone lines at your home or office, get more efficient use from your existing one. The Fax Line Manager by Technology Concepts allows you to effectively channel transmissions to all the communications devices in your home or office using a single phone line. This sophisticated voice/data switch detects and routes voice calls, facsimile messages, and computer modem connections. It will also save you money by eliminating the need for a dedicated fax line.

Automatic Fax Switcher

Fax Switcher allows you to share one line between phone, fax, and modem. It automatically distinguishes voice and fax calls, and gives voice priority. Remote or local programming from any Touch-Tone telephone allows you to enable or disable fax function and answering machine function, or activate or deactivate password feature. It plugs into any standard telephone jack. Available for $79.95 from Reliable Home Office at 800 869-6000.

Fax Booster

An affordable alternative to buying a new state-of-the-art fax machine is Boomerang, a fax booster for your existing machine.

It allows you to retrieve or forward your faxes from anywhere in the world. When you arrive at your destination, you can instruct the Boomerang remote to start forwarding all your incoming faxes to a fax machine accessible to you wherever you are. Boomerang can even signal a pager whenever a fax arrives. A hard copy will be waiting for you at your home-based machine.

Rather than waiting by the machine for a fax to go through, Boomerang will send a fax to as many machines as you want, anywhere in the world, one right after the other. If the receiving fax is busy, Boomerang stores the outgoing document in its memory and retransmits it automatically at a later time—so your machine isn't tied up. This delayed transmission allows you to take advantage of cheaper rates or make up for the change in time zones if you want someone across the world to receive a fax at a certain time. You can also schedule your routine outgoing faxes so they go out at night and you can leave your machine open for incoming faxes. If your machine is out of paper, the memory will store the incoming fax. A retrieval feature allows anyone who didn't receive a complete or legible copy to call Boomerang and directly request that the document be transmitted; no need to locate you and ask that the document be resent.

A bulletin board feature is included which allows you to provide up-to-date information to a large group of people. You merely store the information you want to distribute and anyone with access to a fax can call and request the information.

Boomerang is the equivalent of adding a one-megabyte hard drive to your fax and is available for $399 from Comtrad Industries at 800 992-2966.

FaxPak

If you've ever had the frustrating experience of trying to decipher or uncurl faxes received in expensive thermal paper, you'll appreciate the FaxPak. A separate unit that connects between your computer and printer, it enables you to receive incoming faxes and print them out on your plain-paper laser or dot matrix printer. FaxPak has its own internal memory and works independently of the computer, storing up to forty pages when the printer is off, busy, or out of paper. It will resume once the printer is ready again. FaxPak also offers a built-in voice/fax switch to route incoming calls to the proper device.

Fax this book

Almost all faxes are sent with a cover sheet consisting of transmittal information on company letterhead or an abbreviated version thereof. Although we realize the importance of being businesslike, we also recognize the importance of being human. People like a personal touch and they like humor that isn't offensive. Why not use some of the clever fax cover letters available or create your own, depending on the circumstances?

Workman Publishing offers over one hundred fax cover sheets for a variety of situations in a book entitled *Fax This Book*. The publisher and author, John Caldwell, consent to unlimited photocopying of individual pages by the original purchaser of the book if copied in their entirety and used solely for the pur-chaser's own facsimile transmissions. The *FunnyFax* book also contains over one hundred cover sheets and is available from the Harriet Carter catalog, Dept. 34, North Wales, PA, or call 215 361-5151.

For $10 you'll get a lot of laughs and, just maybe, a returned call from someone who has been avoiding you. Some of the cover sheets offer clever ways to ask for an appointment and just might break down the walls you haven't been able to get over with a phone call to a secretary. If your approach can make a secretary laugh you'll have a better chance of getting through than if you try to trick your way past her.

How to get the fax

Your guide to fax broadcast and fax response services:

MarketFax	914 478-5900
AT&T Easylink Services	800 242-6005—FAXsolutions, FAX catalog
Sprint	800 877-1272—SprintFax, Document on Demand
MCI	800 955-3329—MCI Broad-cast, MCI Fax Reply

Ameritech	800 343-8200—Faxtra, Faxtra on Demand
US West	800 945-9494—US West Broadcast Fax, FaxRequest
Xpedite	800 966-3297—PC-FaxCast
Newport Firstfax	800 825-5515—FirstFax Broadcast, FirstFax on Request
Brooktrout Technology	800 333-5274—FlashFAX
ComArt International	800 FAX-DEMO—Faxcess
Copia	708 924-3030—FaxFacts
Eden Technology	309 862-1804—Phoneoffice
FaxBack	800 FAX-BACK
Fax Quest	800 925-7626 or 415 563-0155—RoboFax-EZ
Hello Direct	408 972-1061—RoboFax-EZ
Ibex	800 289-9998—FactsLine
Novacore Technologies	508 371-2424—Novafax
Nuntius Corporation	314 947-1710—CommandFax
Ricoh	800 241-RFMS—FMS1000
Spectrafax	800 833-1329—Special Request
Valley Infosystems	800 769-9147—FactsLine
Voicelink	708 866-0404—FaxlinkPRO

Magazines offering more information about fax-on-demand are:

Voice Processing magazine, P. O. Box 6016, Duluth, MN 55806-9792, 218 723-9200, fax 218 723-9437.

InfoText, Interactive Telephone Applications, Peter Meade, Editor, 34700 Coast Highway, #309, Capistrano Beach, CA 92624, 714 493-2434, fax 714 493-3018.

153

Contact a few of the service providers and talk to service reps or marketing specialists about your product and how the fax can multiply your efforts. You'll be surprised what they can do for you.

Part III

How Technology Is Changing
the Way We Work

Chapter 12

World Without Wires
(Wireless Communications)

"Modems are going mobile. So pull the plug, hit the road, and stay in touch."

—Cathy Madison[1]

Have you heard the latest one about the traveling salesmen? Their company went wireless and sales productivity increased 15 percent. Selling cycles are shrinking. They're closing more sales with less paperwork. Office operations have been streamlined.

Will this happen for everyone? Will wireless communication automatically upgrade your sales or service? Not necessarily. Potential users must have a need. Companies don't implement wireless data solution because it's "whiz-bang high-tech." The payback must be there.

Wireless communications play the utility role. Like electricity, it's invisible. You don't buy it, as you would a product, you use it. After Thomas Edison commercialized electricity, the "application," such as a light bulb or toaster, had to be invented. To operate on wireless, you first need an application, which resides in the subscriber device, such as a hand-held terminal or laptop, as well as in a host, which delivers business functionality.

Wireless mobile communications products will lead us into the era of anytime/anywhere communications. All you need is one or more of these wireless high-tech gizmos: pager, personal data assistant (PDA), personal intelligent communicator (PIC), laptop, or hand-held wireless phone plus a wireless data modem and application software that can function over a wireless network.

Whether in a building, on the street, or in a vehicle, two-way, wireless data communication gives its users freedom to communicate efficiently with computers and people—instantly, nationwide, from practically anywhere at anytime. You'll have the power to be more productive.

If computers themselves are portable, reason the technology experts, then computing functions should be portable, too. Sales execs ought not to be on their knees in hotel rooms, trying to hook their modem into the phone jack. Radio modems are particularly useful for sales execs who need access to customer files and up-to-the-minute pricing and inventory information—or electronic messaging.

Wireless data transmission is expected to be the "killer application" of the '90s, doing for mobile messaging what the spreadsheet did for the PC. According to the Yankee Group, a respected consulting firm in the wireless data industry, 4 million salespeople "already carry portable computers and access corporate systems via wireline connections."[2] The $500 million wireless data market is projected to double by 1996 and reach $3.8 billion by 2001, with 10 million subscribers.

How does wireless help you close the sale?

Wireless data communications networks give you information when and where you need it. No more chasing down telephones, playing telephone tag, constantly calling the office, or looking for an outlet or phone jack. If you need to confirm pricing, inventory, or check on your customer's open orders, press two or three buttons on your laptop and send the question wirelessly to your company's host computer. Moments later, you've got the information you need.

Compare this speed and convenience with downloading your notebook computer every day. Information is not twenty-four hours old, it's fresh and instantaneous. This is important because often inventories fluctuate by the hour, even by the minute. Regardless of where you are, sitting in an airport terminal or a customer's waiting room, you can access critical information when you need it.

While a fax machine is fast, it's limited. It's only one-way. You don't know when you'll get an answer. With wireless data communications, your request goes straight to the host computer and a reply comes back in seconds. You can tell your customer, "I have it now at this special price." Cellular offers two-way voice interaction, but you still have the extra step of asking someone at your office to answer your questions—rather than tapping into the computer directly yourself. By answering all your customers' questions during the interview, they don't have time to talk to a competitor or change their minds.

Benefits of wireless data communication

- Sales reps can contact their technical team to resolve issues right on the spot, allowing them to accelerate the sales process

- Engineers can instantly alert sales representatives of problems, so they are never blindsided

- Sales reps can be proactive, forewarning a customer of any potential difficulty, even before the client is aware it exists

- Special pricing matters can be addressed with sales management immediately, moving the sale closer to final stages

- Scheduling meetings can happen in seconds

- Sales representatives can discuss strategies with peers and their managers

- E-mail can be assessed and responded to wherever you are

One salesperson told us his hectic route required thirty daily stops. After each sales call he had to find a phone to place his orders before he went to the next call. Since he started using wireless, he says he saves an hour of lost selling time each day.

Wilson Sporting Goods Company went wireless to maintain its competitive edge in product design and customer support. Wilson knew that companies that could keep shelves stocked and retailers satisfied would reign supreme. The challenge was keeping an accurate read on fluctuating stock levels.

Although Wilson's sales representatives could access inventory using their laptops, information was updated only when reps dialed the home office computer at the end of the day. Warehouse inventories of volleyballs, tennis racquets, and golf clubs changed by the minute. Peak buying seasons were particularly challenging. Lacking accurate, up-to-the-minute information, representatives committed delivery dates to retailers when products weren't always available.

Wilson was determined to maintain its edge and sought the velocity of a wireless data solution with ARDIS. Today, Wilson's sales organization uses laptops and radio frequency (RF) modems to communicate over the ARDIS network.

Sales reps check and verify inventory levels on the spot, face-to-face with their customers. In seconds, a delivery date is confirmed. With a quick push of a button, the customer's order is sent to the home office and inventory levels are readjusted automatically. All information is up-to-the-second accurate.

Wilson's customers have been impressed. "Staying ahead in retail is tough," says David Lumley, vice president of Golf Sales & Service. "With ARDIS, our salespeople have discovered they have more time to sell. Most significantly, our customers have noticed a difference in how quickly we're able to commit to delivery on our products."

Empowered with wireless, Wilson's competitive spirit and drive toward excellence has kept them number one—on the shelves, on the court, on the golf course—and most of all, with their customers.

Some companies need wireless to overcome a competitive disadvantage. Transportation clients can instantly track packages and improve pick-up and delivery reliability. Field service organizations use wireless to hold down costs while growing volumes and margins.

Avis car rental uses wireless communications to offer their Preferred Service which allows frequent customers to go directly to the car, completely bypassing the rental counter. "Your wireless vendor becomes your business partner," says Grace Dieterich, systems manager for Avis, "one who will share your philosophy for quality and system integrity." By combining ARDIS radio network, the Avis Wizard network, and the mobile data terminals, Avis designed a software application their drivers would find user-friendly and efficient. Making Wizard wireless has reaped many rewards.

WOW, or Wizard On Wheels, is now successfully rolled out to sixteen major airport locations, with more than 175 remote mobile data terminals operational. Pleased customers remark on rapid service and convenience. Most significantly, Avis has surpassed its original marketing goal. "We've more than doubled our Preferred Customer base in the past year," states Dieterich. "Wireless technology helped make our goal a reality."[3]

Cellular was the first phase of the wireless revolution; the second is mobile data, which provides reliable two-way communications for laptops, palmtops, and new personal digital assistants (PDAs). As with cellular technology, the key to radio modems is not the product itself but the service provider. The choice of a service provider may depend on your home computer and E-mail systems.

Information highway construction zone

Much development is going into MANs (metropolitan area networks). Users pay subscription costs, plus fees for data packets sent, no matter how many tries or how long it takes. Two wireless data networks exist in the United States right now. The first one is RAM Mobile Data network, which uses a public networking technology called Mobitex. Started in 1991, RAM is already in 6,300 cities. The second is ARDIS, which is based on technology developed by Motorola and IBM. ARDIS has more than 35,000 subscribers and covers 95 percent of the United States, in 400 metropolitan areas and more than 10,700 cities and towns.

Pricing varies; look for packages and promotions. RAM, for example, charges a $50-per-terminal registration fee, plus $25 per month, plus between 4 cents (2 to 55 bytes) and 12.5 cents (512 bytes, or about a paragraph) per packet during prime time (6:00 A.M. to 8:00 P.M. every day).

Information systems, from PC to mainframe, can be connected to ARDIS via radio modem, dial-up, dedicated leased line, or through a variety of value-added networks. Virtually any information system can be extended to the wireless world because ARDIS supports a variety of industry standard connectivity protocols. Service and customer support is available twenty-four hours a day, seven days a week with a proven decade-long track record. ARDIS currently serves more than thirty-two thousand users from more than fifty Fortune 500 companies.

McCaw Cellular, GTE, and seven other cellular operators are developing standards for a new Cellular Digital Packet Data (CDPD) system, which will allow data packets to be interspersed with voice and to take advantage of idle time on existing cellular networks. CDPD makes possible the delivery of voice and data on a single device and can be laid over existing analog cellular networks. Specialized mobile radio (SMR) will be brought to us by Nextel Communications Inc. with the help of Motorola. Nextel is enhancing and converting to digital the two-way radio dispatching service now used by taxis and trucks.

Motorola has joined forces with McDonald Douglas Corporation to launch its Iridium Project, a wireless telecommunications system. This $3.37 billion Iridium network is based on sixty-six low-earth-orbiting satellites interconnected through cross-links to provide complete coverage of the earth. McDonnell Douglas will launch eight Delta II rockets over two years beginning in 1996 to place forty communications satellites in orbit. An international consortium of telecommunications and other companies are funding the project.

This worldwide telecommunications network will enable you to send and receive phone calls, faxes, pages, and data anywhere in the world from a hand-held wireless phone-type unit. Unlike cellular phone service, you'll have one number that will be good no matter where you are, since your calls will be transmitted from satellite, not cells. The system should be operational by 1998. Completion of this task will boost the wireless wave even higher and make room for a whole new generation of modems.[4]

Anytime, anywhere, where do you begin?

Depending on what kind you choose, wireless modems are available from the manufacturer through service providers in computer stores. All modems hook into a computer's RS-232 serial port (they work on any type of computer). Motorola makes the InfoTAC, dubbed a personal data communicator because it also is a stand-alone device capable of receiving, storing, and automatically acknowledging messages. You can preprogram one-key responses, like yes/no or "okay to proceed." It lists at $1,350, fits in your hand, and weighs just more than a pound. Batteries last about eight hours.

Look for package deals, which include the modem as well as the mailbox and communication software. Ericsson GE makes the popular Mobidem family of modems, such as the new Mobidem AT, similar to Motorola's in size, weight, and stand-alone function. It has only two keys; one for on/off, and the other to save power. Some of these products are sold at retail under the Intel name. RadioMail also sells them in package deals ranging from $795 to $995; the latter includes a Hewlett-Packard 95LX palmtop computer. Also consider new computers already equipped with wireless modem capabilities.

The Ubiquity 2000 is the first modem approved by the Federal Communications Commission for cellular digital packet data (CDPD). It sends voice and fax data over cellular phone links. Brought to you by PCSI of San Diego for $1,500, it will fit inside an IBM ThinkPad laptop. Look for prices to go down when the cellular system is upgraded.

For one-stop shopping, investigate RadioMail. The San Mateo, California, company charges a $99 activation fee and $89 per month for unlimited wireless messaging, including network fees. Users get an electronic mailbox and access to Internet, which links company and institutional E-mail systems all over the world. If your company isn't on the Internet, you can arrange to hook in for a minimal extra charge.

MobileComm, a BellSouth Company, now has a lease package which includes an Apple Newton, a Motorola pager, and Apple Wireless Messaging for around $50.00 per month, based on a two-year lease. Nationwide coverage starts at around $70.00 per month. With this system, you will be able to store ideas, create memos, send faxes, and arrange your schedule. With the pager card, messages can be transmitted directly from a PC to you. Call 800 474-MESG.

Even if you can't yet afford to communicate seamlessly from coffee shops or tunnels, taxis or airplanes, with no roaming charges, pay attention to this field. As usage goes up—and it will—hardware and service prices will decline dramatically.

"In today's business world, conquering the competition requires more than traditional communications methods," says Lesley Berkshire, ARDIS manager of Market Development. "We believe that ARDIS can mean the difference between a closed door and a closed sale." If you are interested in how ARDIS and sales force automation can work in your organization, contact Lesley Berkshire at 708 913-4232.

Chapter 13

Home Alone?
(Telecommuting)

"They can live where they choose, set their own hours, and, when the spirit moves, kick off their shoes. For 670,000 telecommuting salespeople, work is no longer the same old routine. On-line and off-site, these home-aloners may form the fastest growing subculture in sales today."

—Shane Tritsch[1]

Telepresence

Riding the waves of technology, telecommunications consultant and speaker Peter G. W. Keen used to hide his Virgin Island location from clients. Now he includes a photograph of his Caribbean view on his business card. Author of *Shaping the Future: Business Design Through Information Technology* and *Every Manager's Guide to Information Technology*, Keen says telecommuting has allowed him to double his income with far less work. "Every time we reduced the head count, our productivity and happiness went up significantly." Now his overhead is reduced to the cost of communications and travel which run between $10,000 and $15,000 per month including $2,000 for phone and $2,500 for MCI Mail and other on-line services. But these expenditures are far less than fifty-five salaries and rented office space in New York.[2]

Although his telecommuting began as a wager with some dinner guests, some of his clients believe his work has improved dramatically since moving to the island and is the most innovative he's ever done. Keen focuses on creating organizational simplicity by redefining business processes and helping companies implement information technologies. A living example of his own philosophy, he states that managers with the best insight about the relationship between business processes and technology will be the winners; those following the old strategies and structures will be the losers.

When a corporate customer calls AT&T's Paul Schouppe to inquire about long-distance service, the phone does not ring at the company's Wayne, Pennsylvania, branch office, as it would have in the old days. Instead, it rings at Schouppe's house, one hundred miles away in rural Monroe County, in the heart of Pennsylvania's Pocono Mountains. There the AT&T account executive can field calls, log pertinent data into his personal computer, print out a price quote on his laser printer, and fax it to the customer on the spot. For all the customer knows, Schouppe could be sitting in a fluorescent-lit cubicle, clad in a coat and tie, and flanked by AT&T colleagues. In fact, he is in the study adjacent to his living room, wearing chinos and a sport shirt. He is kept company by the family dog and cat and by the white-tailed deer that wander into the yard to nibble on apples and crusts of bread.[3]

Moved out of the branch office nearly two years ago, Schouppe is one of AT&T's new breed of sales representatives who work from a "virtual office," a term that refers more to high-tech geewhizzery than to an actual place. Schouppe's virtual office is really nothing more than a telephone, personal computer, modem, printer, and fax. The equipment is set up in his home, but a laptop computer, cellular phone, and portable printer enable him to get virtual almost anyplace, from a roadside rest stop to a customer's office.

The fact that Schouppe's geographic location is transparent to his customers proves he has achieved "telepresence," a dimension-bender of a notion that suggests you can exist just about anywhere electronically—provided you have the technology. Linked to the branch office by phone, fax, and modem, Schouppe can perform all the duties he once did at the office as effectively as if he were actually there. And he is able to serve his customers more effectively because he can travel to their premises often in a matter of minutes rather than hours or the next day.[4]

Just give us the fax

Welcome to the brave new world of telecommuting, coming soon to a home near you—if it hasn't already arrived. The benefits of telecommuting—increased productivity, reduced stress, less traffic, and better air quality—have been known for years, but businesses have been slow to adopt telecommuting policies.

A 1993 survey by the Society for Human Resource Management revealed that 42 percent of companies with more than five thousand employees have "work at home" programs. According to the New York–based research firm Link Resources, 39 million Americans performed work at home during 1992 (up 56 percent from 25 million in 1988) with 12 million of them operating a business full-time and an equal number running a sideline pursuit in their spare time. Over 7.5 million salaried employees "tele-commuted" full-time from their residences in 1993 and an additional 8.6 million staffers regularly took work home as an alternative to longer hours at the office. Figures also show that the number of telecommuters is growing at an annual rate of 15 percent. Fifty-four percent of telecommuters were men, and the large majority (74 percent) of the telecommuting work force were knowledge/information workers. Telecommuters reported reduced commuting costs and travel time as their largest benefits, while employers benefitted from office space savings, reduced utility costs, and lower maintenance costs.[5]

In 1992 some 670,000 salespeople telecommuted, which is to say they worked at home rather than at a company office at least part-time during normal business hours, according to Link Resources. That figure grew a whopping 81 percent from 1991, making telecommuters the fastest growing segment among all salespeople who work at home. LINK Resources estimates that the growth rate of telecommuters will be 20 percent by 1996. In all, 34 million salespeople worked at home in 1992, up about 10 percent from the previous year. That total includes corporate salespeople who work at home full-time, those who work at home after regular business hours, and primary and part-time self-employed salespeople. The $4.5 billion spent on home computers and the $1 billion paid for telephone-answering machines last year included buyers from all of the above groups.[6]

An eco-friendly policy

This explosive growth is happening in part because federal clean air regulations will soon require businesses in cities with air-quality problems to reduce employee car trips to the office. Local regulations are already in effect in Los Angeles, and telecommuting is an eco-friendly way to comply. In a California Chamber of Commerce address, Former President George Bush said, "If only 5 percent of the commuters in Los Angeles County telecommuted one day each week, they'd . . . keep 47,000 tons of pollutants from entering the atmosphere."[7]

Disaster strikes

In January 1994 the Los Angeles area earthquake caused such extreme delays in commuting that Pacific Bell received almost two thousand calls regarding setting up telecommuting programs. Telebusiness centers leasing desk space and telecommuting equipment suddenly flourished, enabling commuters to become telecommuters. About sixty thousand new telecommuters were added to the existing six hundred thousand, and they expect to have 1.5 million by the turn of the century. Pacific Bell is offering new telecommuters free installation of business telephone lines, voice mail, and other services. It also has set up a $1 million program to lend telephone, fax machines, and modems to telecommuters.[8]

"The earthquake has made companies totally rethink the value of telecommuting," says Jim Backer, marketing director for the Valencia Corporate Telecommuting Center. "Previously, companies liked having employees in the office and around the building." Now, he says, "they realize people can be more effective at work—no matter where that is—if they don't have to spend so much time on the road."[9]

Homework can be fun

The growth of telecommuting probably would have happened without statutory impetus and the earthquake disaster, simply because the advantages of home-based selling are irresistible. By turning to telecommuting, companies such as AT&T, Hewlett-Packard, GTE, and Bell Atlantic are able to eliminate office space and slash real estate expenditures. Employees, meanwhile, are relieved of the hassle, expense, and wasted time of commuting. Companies that offer the flexibility and convenience of working from home can find it easier to attract and retain valuable employees. The companies also benefit from having workers who are often more productive and better able to serve their customers.

Technology moves in mysterious ways. Sally and Glenn Priest are a two-telecommuter family who say that the tools of modern telecommuting have allowed them to find not only new work but also themselves. Computer and communications technologies have allowed them to live on Vashon Island outside Seattle where they've "discovered a part of themselves that has nothing to do with technology—something low-tech and human. 'I've learned how to be a father and a husband,' Glenn Priest explains. 'And how to enjoy my life.'"

Sally operates a legal education seminar group out of their home, commuting to Seattle by ferry every few days. Via computer modem, fax, telephone, and on-line services, Glenn works as Sony Electronics' educational systems sales representative for the Pacific Northwest territory, handling most of the contact work and prospecting from their island home. "I'm not a different person," Priest says, "I've let myself reach my true potential."[10]

Telecommuting potholes

"Our fears about at-home workers were that they'd be sipping a martini instead of working," recalled Gary Gagliardi, CEO of FourGen Software, before he gave it a try. Initially Gagliardi required his home workers to keep time sheets and carefully monitored their output. When productivity increased by 25 percent, Gagliardi eliminated the time sheets and sent seven more workers home to telecommute. The key is communication, he says. "We're on E-mail all day. And everyone attends our weekly meetings."[11]

Of course, working from home also has its share of trade-offs. It challenges communications by reducing face-to-face contact at the office. It isolates employees from peers and superiors. And it has the potential to disrupt households by eliminating the separation between work and family life. Some people even admit to not getting dressed all day and having problems staying away from the refrigerator and TV. Several regulations govern telecommuters—such as whether they are exempt or nonexempt employees. Workers' compensation insurance isn't always easy to get and other benefits are sometimes limited.

Despite these concerns, the growing ranks of "open-collar" salespeople are proving resoundingly that you *can* go home again.

Wiring your home

Selling from a home office is not a radically new concept. What has changed in recent years is the level of sophistication home-based offices have attained. Now a room outfitted with the latest computer hardware and software can pack the kind of productive wallop that only a company office once could.

"People now have the technological capability to be as effective out of their homes as they'd be at corporate headquarters," says Paul Edwards, author, with his wife, Sarah, and Laura Clampitt Douglas of *Getting Business to Come to You* and other books about home businesses.

The big guns in the home office arsenal include high-powered, low-priced workstations; high-bandwidth communication lines that allow heavy volume, computer-to-computer data transfers and simultaneous remote access to multiple computer systems; and sophisticated software that enables a home-based sales rep to track market trends, account history, and product information. Fax machines, cellular phones, and telephone services such as voice-mail and three-way calling help bridge the communications gap, along with personal digital assistants, which combine phone, fax, and computing in one unit.

The upshot of all this gadgetry is that information, the lifeblood of selling, is infinitely mobile and accessible. And that's why for some salespeople, working from home makes more and more sense.

"Now a sales rep can talk to a customer from home and have access to all the resources of the headquarters office—and at no impact to the customer," says Kevin Matlock, a regional sales manager for Hewlett-Packard. "There's no performance limitation because a person is at home."[12]

In fact, the National Center for Labor Analysis found that 67 percent said their productivity increased as a result of working at home. Sixty-two percent of home telecommuters complained of interruptions and distractions at the company office. The National Center for Policy Analysis conducted a survey which revealed only 40 percent of telecommuters started their workday at the conventional hours. More than half worked late at night.

Working where you live

To Patrick Zabala, Interstate 10 in and out of Los Angeles had become a sort of asphalt Hotel California. He could get on anytime he liked, but he could never leave—or so it seemed. As Zabala recalls, "You'd come down the ramp at 5:00 P.M. and park on the freeway." He spend four hours each day commuting to and from his job at GTE Telephone Operations in Thousand Oaks. In the evenings he limped home, a twitching, exhausted mess.

"I had zero energy," he says. "My eyes would be red and irritated. I was neglecting my kids and wife. Friday nights were out as far as doing anything. I just went to bed." Zabala had almost no time for friends or household chores either. He even gave up his hobby of building antique street rods in his garage.

So when his boss offered him a chance to commute via electronic freeway, Zabala jumped. Working as a "smart park" consultant from an office in his home, Zabala now sells businesses on the idea of tapping into GTE's networks of fiber-optic phone lines, known as smart parks. He goes into Thousand Oaks once every week or two, but otherwise sticks close to home.

The payoffs have been dramatic, both professionally and personally. Zabala has developed stronger relationships with his customers because he sees them two or three times a week from home rather than once a month from headquarters. As a result, he says, "I have been able to develop sales opportunities that we would have missed altogether if I were stationed in Thousand Oaks." He also is able to "sleep in" until 6:00 A.M. (as opposed to 4:30 in his commuting days), cook dinner for his family, and even have lunch in the park occasionally with his kids. He's also returned to his old hobby. His new project: a 1928 Ford Model A sedan.

As Zabala and others have learned, working at home fosters greater control over one's time, affording better balance between personal and professional obligations.[13]

Living where you want

People who work out of their homes have flexibility in where they live as well. In 1989 John Harper had just finished building his dream house near the Intracoastal Waterway in Ponte Vedra Beach, Florida when he landed a job at Menlo Care, a manufacturer of medical devices. Problem was, Menlo Care's offices were three thousand miles away, in Menlo Park, California. Harper wanted the job, but didn't want to leave his house or uproot his family. His solution is to commute to California half of each month and telecommute from a home office the rest of the time. In 1991, Harper became vice president of sales and marketing. He gets to have his house and live in it, too.

Richard Wattam's situation was just the opposite. When he became a senior technical sales rep for a division of Miles, Inc.—a maker of blood protein—Wattam's supervisor told him he could live anywhere in his Eastern U.S. territory. So Wattam, who lived in Rockville, Maryland, rounded up his family and moved to Disney World—Orlando, that is, swimming pool and . . . Goofy. Wattam chose Orlando because his wife had relatives there and because he could afford a bigger house and yard. Wattam spends a lot of time on the road, but he also works quite a bit from his home office and enjoys the pleasures of a Sunbelt lifestyle. In fact, he hasn't regretted the move for a moment.

John Datsopoulos doesn't regret his move either. In fact, he's positively ebullient about it. As a former employee of Firestone Tire and Rubber and Black and Decker, he has worked in office buildings in big cities from Hong Kong to London. What he always longed for was the quiet charm and clean air of his native Missoula, Montana. Now, as an international management consultant and manufacturer's rep for U.S. medical equipment makers, he is living his dream in Missoula. He spends most of his time working out of an office in a wing of his home, surrounded by artifacts from places he's worked around the world. Out the window he can see a creek, spruce trees, and the peaks of the Rocky Mountains. He can also jump on a plane and be in Seattle in an hour, and from there reach the Far East, where he does most of his business.

"I get into big cities often on business and enjoy them," Datsopoulos says. "But when it takes two hours to go a couple of blocks and you start choking on the pollution, you realize how good you have it back here with the fresh air, mountains, lakes, and no traffic or crime. As you get older, these are the things you enjoy."

Datsopoulos's verdict on working at home? "I would never work in an office again if I could help it."[14]

One of our favorite telecommuters is Leanna Lewis. She lives on a yacht named Cheers in Alameda, California and sells cruises on luxury yachts to corporate clients. When she finds it necessary to go to her office on San Francisco's Pier 39, she takes the ferry. Way to go, Leanna![15]

The bottom line

Jack Niles, president of Southern California's Telecommuting Advisory Council and the man credited with coining the word "telecommute" in the '70s claims electronic commuting provides companies a net savings of $8,000 to $9,000 per employee per year, mostly in improved productivity and reduced turnover.[16] They also save on overhead and office space and might find it easier to attract employees and salespeople with this flexible arrangement.

The State of California projected that the amount of money California could save per home telecommuter is estimated to be as high as 71 percent of each worker's salary. Included in this estimate are savings from increased productivity, more output per employee, higher quality of output, fewer sick days, and decreased turnover. It also gives business owners more opportunities to comply with the American Disabilities Act.

For more information about telecommuting, you can subscribe to *Telecommuting Review* and read *Creating a Flexible Workplace* by Barney Olmsted and Suzanne Smith (AMACOM 800 262-9699). The book discusses the management issues raised by telecommuting, job sharing, and part-time workers. It includes clear, helpful charts and work sheets and recommends further resources.[17]

Is telecommuting for everyone? Definitely not. Some salespeople are such social creatures they couldn't exist in isolation. For those, a "virtual water cooler" is in the works, which will probably mean getting together occasionally with their coworkers and socializing.

Chapter 14

Trains, Planes, and Work Stations
(Travel Tips)

"While you are away, movie stars are taking your women. Robert Redford is dating your girlfriend, Tom Selleck is kissing your lady, Bart Simpson is making love to your wife."

—Baghdad Betty
Iraqi radio announcer to Gulf War troops

On the road again . . .

Sales and Marketing Management recently surveyed their readers about their travel time and type of product or service. Sixty percent worked for industrial products companies, 31 percent in services, and 16 percent in consumer businesses. Those in industrial products averaged 28.3 trips per year of 3.4 days each. Those in service travel 25 times per year on trips lasting an average of 3 days. In consumer goods, the numbers were 35.2 trips and 3.2 days for a total of 113.3 days away from home per year. During these trips the time allocated for sales calls was 41 percent in consumer goods, 49 percent in services, and 57 percent in industrial products.[1] That leaves a lot of time for work on the road, in the car, a hotel, airport, or plane.

To make the most productive use of your time out of the office, utilize today's technology and purchase a laptop or notebook computer which runs on batteries for hours, yet has the performance of a desktop computer. Other basic equipment needs include a pager and a cellular phone. Your pager will alert you when you have messages. Call your office for voice mail and then download your E-mail messages into your computer.

An optional piece of equipment you will find helpful is a notebook printer. If you don't want to bother with a printer and need a hard copy of your computer input, plug the modem into a phone system, make a local phone call, and fax the document to yourself at your hotel. You can attach a portable fax to your car phone if you travel long distances and need to get information frequently between destinations.

Portable equipment can be used in unlimited ways—checking on inventory while on the sales call or creating and printing out a customized presentation, bid, or sales agreement. Make notes on each sales call and write thank-you letters to customers after you leave their office while the information is still fresh in your mind. Your laptop computer can be used in your car, on a plane, in hotels, in customers' offices, in a scenic park so you can watch the ducks, or wherever you choose to work.

If you plan to use your computer in your hotel, make sure your travel agent finds out if the hotel's phone system is computer compatible. This is a fairly common problem with hotel-room phones and desk phones, or any phone that is one of many phones hooked to a single trunk line. If anyone else picks up another phone and starts dialing or talking, that will interfere with your transmission. Many hotels have executive/sales areas with special lines that work with computers but most are only open during business hours. Some hotel chains offer PCs and a modem jack in your room.

If you're staying at Holiday Inn, ITT Sheraton Group, Marriott, or Royal Sonesta, ask for "Corporate Class" and expect an in-room business center including a desk; IBM compatible 386 PC with Lotus 1-2-3, Microsoft Word, Windows, WordPerfect for Windows, and Prodigy; fax machine; two-line speaker phone; and a modem hookup. Also check out Summerfield Suites, Residence Inns, Homewood Suites, and Hawthorne Suites.

There's a six-ounce device that will take control of any multiple-line phone jack and turn it into a dedicated outlet for modem and fax transmission. Intelemate II, from Datalogic, costs $300 and plugs into any standard telephone wall socket and converts that to a standard Bell RJ-11 single line. Call 800 397-2200.

Talk to AT&T or your phone company about their travel services. AT&T offers TeleTravel which features many of the regular services plus three-way conference calls, speed dialing, itemized charges by client, the capability to send and receive recorded messages, your own voice mailbox, on-line interpreters, flight, weather, and sports information, etc. Call 800 544-2222.

If you're on the road and aren't staying at a hotel and need office equipment you don't have, try one of Kinko's six hundred copy centers located throughout the United States. Their ad reads, "Until there's a copy-color-oversize-fax-computer-mail drop-binding-delivery-to-your-door machine, there's us." They're open seven days a week, twenty-four hours a day. For the location nearest you, call 800 743-COPY. Other full service office centers are available in many cities whose services include renting equipment or using it in their office, or having it done for you by a secretarial service.

Your ticket's in the E-mail

Computer literate salespeople are reducing their busywork by making flight arrangements via E-mail. Some computer programs list only flight options that comply with corporate travel guidelines. Consolidated Rail Corp.'s E-mail system lists hotels at which the company has negotiated rates, and discount airfares for key travel cities. In addition, "we don't have secretaries typing and distributing stupid memos of itineraries and flight options anymore," says Michael Kabo, Conrail's director of administrative services. While the savings are substantial, Kabo adds, "We wouldn't know how to calculate the time travelers or secretaries spend on hold with the agency or typing, not to mention the cost of paper and distribution."

Other firms, using E-mail in an advanced system called Resolution from TravelNet Inc., are documenting savings as they automatically book travelers on airlines offering the best prices, says John Shoolery, president of the Santa Barbara, California, software firm that offers the service. And some just offer computerized travel planning because it's part of their corporate culture.[2]

In the air . . .

Coming soon to an airline seat near you are fold-up display screens, modem hookups, real-time financial news, and other telecommunication attractions dedicated to in-flight business output. USAir, United, American, and Delta already offer GTE Airfones. Once it is converted to a digital signal, users will be able to use it to transmit data by plugging into a connection in the armrest. Also coming soon will be connecting cables for using your laptop on the plane. Satellite communications gear allows in-flight use of faxes and modems.

If you want to take a plane and the disk too, Lufthansa's Lauda-Air offers on-board Apple Powerbooks for your flight to Vienna. British Airways and Swiss Air offer fax services while in the wild blue yonder. Some airlines preassign a phone number to you if you're in first class.

According to Business Traveler, twenty-one of the top fifty-three airlines will have individual seat video screens installed in 1994. Interactive video systems featuring in-flight shopping and on the ground theater ticket booking are coming soon to an airline near you. If these services are important to you when you fly, check with your travel agent for an update on which airlines have what.

Gradually more airlines are becoming aware of travelers' technological needs. However, they are still a little uncomfortable with what all that electronic equipment might be doing to delicate aircraft instruments. If you are asked not to use your equipment during takeoff, landing, or below ten thousand feet, don't think it's cute to sneak behind their backs and use your phone or computer. The life they're trying to save may be your own.

For those who travel on corporate planes not yet fitted with phones, look into the Jetfone TD-3000 by Terra. If you have $7,500 to spend call 505 884-2321. Additional benefits such as a digital signal and the capacity to send and receive faxes are available on Flitefone 800 by Global Wulfsberg Systems. However, you will need to make lots of phone calls to make it cost effective. Call 206 865-3711 and be prepared to spend $35,000.[3]

Charge me, please

If you've ever tried to recharge your computer battery in the shaver outlet of the airplane restroom, or wandered around an airport looking for a place to plug in your computer, you will be happy to know that American Airlines will test retrofitting some planes with alternating current charging stations which, thankfully, are outside the restrooms.

When you're not on the plane, of course, keep your battery charged up by plugging into an electric outlet. For around $100 you can purchase a 110 adapter that plugs into your cigarette lighter in your car and will save computer batteries or allow you to charge it while driving. To be on the safe side, always carry extra battery packs and a charger. Maybe someday soon cars will come equipped with multiple cigarette lighters so you can keep all your mobile office equipment charged up while traveling.

Airline schedules

Is there anyone out there who travels by plane on a regular basis and doesn't carry an OAG Pocket Flight Guide with you? If you don't, stop complaining to us about standing in long lines trying to get rerouted when your plane is cancelled or the runway snowed in. For $86 per year you can avoid standing in line at the airport waiting for information by pulling out your own flight guide and high-tailing it over to that terminal before the rest of the crowd discovers that option. While you're walking, use your cellular phone to call the airline for a reservation. Then call 800 DIAL-OAG to subscribe. One of the fringe benefits includes *Frequent Flyer*, a magazine full of travel tips.

American Express offers a SkyGuide for $45 per year which includes information on over forty thousand direct flights, a Connections Guide, and a frequent flyer Partners-At-A-Glance Guide. For more information call 800 678-6738.

User friendly airports . . .

Take advantage of your waiting time at the airport by using their business center or frequent flier room. Most frequent flier VIP suites in airports are equipped with fax machines, computer hookups, and sometimes computers. However, if you've ever tried to use one when the airport is snowed in, you know you have to get in line.

If you're Stranded at O'Hare, ask to buy the book by the same title for $9.95. The book tells you where to stash your bags and places to visit near the airport.

Airports are becoming more traveler-friendly, offering a wide variety of services to meet travelers' needs. London's Heathrow and Gatwick airports offer their British Airways ClubWorld and first class passengers shower facilities in a private lounge. You can take a shower, grab some breakfast and have your clothes pressed before your first meeting.

Tokyo's Haneda International Airport now resembles a mall with fifty-one retail stores and kiosks and thirty-two service facilities including post office, medical clinic, brokerage office, hair cutting facilities, meeting rooms, and a business center with laptops available for use on their premises without charge.

Where there's smoke . . .

You might sleep a little sounder if you pack a travel smoke alarm. Battery powered with a low-battery signal, its eighty-five-decibel horn will make you think an eighteen-wheeler rolled into your room. It affixes to any surface with a suction cup. Available from Orvis (800 541-3541) for $17.50.

Security

Female travelers might want to check with Express Reservations at 800 356-1123 to check out some of their concerns regarding services offered by various hotels, including the part of town they're in.

If you want to make a pickpocket wish he had taken the day off, pay $90 for a "Colloc" wallet. Made of plastic and light-weight steel, it opens without problem with a combination lock.

If a thief tries to pry it open, however, everything in it—including credit cards—turns blue. Call 800 545-4808 to order and register a serial number so the wallet will be returned to you if it's lost.

Your attacker may have to put in a request for sick pay if you order The Hidden Edge for $49.50. Cleverly designed to look like a cellular phone, it contains a mini-canister of pepper spray which will give the mugger thirty minutes to wish he had never messed with you. To call attention to his plight it comes equipped with a 130-decibel siren. Call 800 513-1984 and hope you never need to use it.

If in spite of your precautions someone reached under the restroom cubicle and stole your laptop computer, be sure to file a stolen computer report with Nacomex's Stolen Computer Registry at 212 777-1291 or AmCoEx at 800 786-0717. Because they are a hot ticket item for thieves and can bring in as much as a used car, we recommend backing up your hard drive on disks and keeping them in a separate location such as your briefcase or purse rather than in your computer carrying case. Before you take that computer on the road, make sure you have written down the make, model, and serial number and put it with your list of valuables for insurance purposes.

It's also a good idea to carry diskettes with you of your software and data, but don't keep them in your computer case in the event it's stolen. And for crucial data you will need on your trip such as your itinerary, phone numbers, and presentation data, make sure you take a hard copy (on paper) in case you run into a multiple-car pileup on the information highway.

If you've heard the numerous horror stories about international business travelers being picked up by people they assumed were their hosts and finding out they had been kidnapped and robbed by thugs, you might want to check out Air Security at 713 977-2204. For 10 percent of what you spend on accommodations and transportation, they will do security checks on hotel rooms, vehicles, drivers, etc.

Better back up than be sorry

Accidents do happen, and you don't want to be victimized by your hard disk crashing when the plane hits an air pocket and all the overhead luggage comes tumbling down. Back up your hard drive on a regular basis, but definitely before you take it with you on a trip. If your data would be nearly impossible to retrieve if lost, back up continually on diskettes. If you've ever experienced the anguish of data that was irretrievably lost, you don't need to be reminded to back up because you already do it as regularly as you wash your hands. Call us paranoid if you want, but as this book reached its final stages, back-up disks were generated every day and kept in separate locations. Those disks went to restaurants, the dentist, or stayed in the car in case of fire or theft at home or in the office.

Also, it's important to back up your hard drive periodically every day as you work rather than wait until the end of the day. You never know when the electricity is going to go out or a computer malfunction will cause you to lose data. Some floppies don't have a very good record for file retention so be especially careful with them.

3M Corporation commissioned a survey by Intelliquest Research of Austin on why people started backing up their data and found the following: computers often are entrusted with material that small businesses can't exist without, yet only 18 percent of small businesses have backup policies. Among those who do back up religiously, 48 percent did so because of the importance of the data, 28 percent had a previous experience of data loss, 15 percent did so because it was a company policy or legal obligation, but 5 percent did so because they did not trust computers. The survey also revealed that destroyed data costs businesses some $4 billion each year, yet few companies have formal back up policies. Call 800 328-9438 for a free copy of 3M's *Data Security Handbook*.

Finding yourself

Okay. We won't tell anyone, but you're lost and have no idea where you are or how to get where you want to go. You're not the first and you won't be the last. Hand held navigation systems are available which will display your exact 3D location, accurate to about one hundred miles. Called Global Positioning Systems (GPS), these little devices which are about the size of your TV remote control are great for hikers, mountain bikers, cross-country skiers, boaters, aviators, backcountry drivers, and salespeople who make calls in remote areas or who get off the beaten track. Ranging in price from $500 to $1700, they can be worth their weight in gold if you find yourself in Death Valley. Read the January 1994 issue of *Popular Mechanics* for a description and evaluation of six of the most popular models.

If you get lost in the city, open your CD-ROM–equipped laptop computer, put in your DeLorme Street Atlas U.S.A., and enter the street address where you are—and up will pop a map of your surroundings. If you aren't lost yet but are on your way to see a client in an unfamiliar city, you can punch in their phone number, zip code, street, or area and a few seconds later find a map of their area on your computer screen. If you need to find the closest gas station, put in The National Yellow Pages Directory and search for one in your map area. It is also available for overseas travel.

To prevent getting lost (especially if you're driving in Tokyo), contact Sony Corp. about its video car-navigation system which blends travel information databases with maps that use satellite signals to pinpoint your exact location. In Japan they have been selling for around $2,500 for eighteen months, but then it's harder to get around in Japan than the United States, according to many. It will also be available on CD-ROM discs on a version called City Streets, produced by Road Scholar Software of Houston, for use on your laptop computer. For $600 you will be able to access 250 U.S. and European cities. (See Chapter 6 on CD-ROMs for other map software.)

What, you forgot your briefcase?

All right, admit it. No one stole it. You forgot your briefcase. Or better yet, you're on vacation and found a ripe prospect so you need a briefcase to look official. Before you go out and buy one you intend to return as soon as the ink is dry on the dotted line, ask your hotel if you can borrow a briefcase and a computer. Some Ritz-Carltons will loan you a fully loaded briefcase. Many hotels will rent computers. Some will even loan you crutches if you "break a leg" as you go for the close.

Global travel

Before you go, contact the international-studies center at Brigham Young University in Provo, Utah. They offer "Culturegrams," four-page reports on more than one hundred areas of the world. They include information about proper greetings, religious customs, eating, gestures, and more. Call 800 528-6279. One costs $3 but purchase two or more and they're $1.50 each.

Buy a copy of Roger Axtel's *Do's and Taboos Around the World* for a complete guide to international correctness. Much of the information was compiled by the Parker Pen Company with offices in 120 countries, with assistance from Brigham Young University. The book covers protocol, customs, etiquette, hand gestures, and body language. Also included is a quick guide to the ways of the world, American jargon, and idioms.

Worldview TripPlan provides a service that will update you on more than 170 cities in the world. They will fax or send on-line information to your computer time-sensitive details such as recommended restaurants in various price ranges, the best way to get to your location from the airport, computer rental outlets, conference facilities, banking, security, business protocol, and translator services. The reports cost between $7 and $15, depending on the information requested. Call 800 638-7799.

Look into a variety of language translators available. Tozai offers a Spanish/English fourteen thousand-word translator for only $16.99. It also includes currency conversion and calculator features.

Franklin's Spanish Master translates over two hundred thousand words and phrases and has a spell checker for written correspondence for around $150.

Heartland offers a couple of translators. The Seiko TR2500 European Translator provides instant access to over eighteen thousand words and phrases in English, Spanish, French, German, and Italian for $38. Or you can choose from four thousand words in fourteen languages including English, French, German, Spanish, Dutch, Italian, Norwegian, Swedish, Finnish, Danish, Czeck, Slovak, Turkish, and Indonesian for $49. To order call 800 966-1233.

For $100 you can put eight languages in your pocket. Translate ten thousand words per language in English, German, French, Spanish, Italian, Polish, Russian, and Dutch by using Sharper Image's 8 Language Translator II. It also gives you 150 useful phrases in each language, home time and alarm, world time for 128 cities, 8 currency conversions, metric, and a 10-digit calculator. You can order it by calling 800 344-4444.

Global software

Bilingual word processing in Spanish and English is available from Road Scholar. More than 1.2 million words are in the program, including idiomatic phrases. It will conjugate twelve thousand verbs in Spanish and thirteen thousand in English. Call 800 243-7623 and ask about Spanish Scholar.

Look into Kanji Word if you need Japanese/English software. Included in the $199 price is a fifty thousand Japanese-English dictionary and sample Japanese documents such as purchase orders, agreements, and invoices. Call Pacific Software at 800 232-3989 to get a sample disc for $20.

Global phone service

"Have I reached the person to whom I am speaking?"
—Lily Tomlin as Ernestine

If you watched the movie *E.T.* you realized he had considerable problems trying to phone home. The phone system on his planet wasn't compatible with ours. While traveling abroad, in many countries you face phone problems that make E.T.'s problems look small. When we speak of culture shock, more than likely it includes phone service.

A friend told us about traveling from Vienna to Budapest late at night by train and trying to make a phone call when she arrived. She didn't have any currency or coins for Hungary and the exchange booths were closed. No one would take Austrian currency or coins but she did find a few taxi drivers who would exchange American dollars for coins for the phone booths. What they didn't tell her was that in Budapest only one out of ten calls actually goes through. The other nine calls drop off into some vacuum in the antiquated phone system equipment and her money only fills up the coin box in the phone booth. Coin return technology hasn't yet arrived in Budapest.

Traveling alone, she wasn't thrilled with walking around the area looking for a phone that worked, not knowing that her chances weren't any greater outside the train station. Much to her amazement, phones were not readily available in the surrounding hotels and businesses. Twenty-seven dollars and two hours later she reached her contact, John Guelian, who, ironically, was a cellular phone distributor in Budapest. She had a new appreciation for his business potential in Budapest.

Salespeople traveling abroad on business are faced with a variety of problems when they try to use American technology. If you're traveling with your laptop computer, take along power transformers so your computer doesn't get fried in a foreign country. And of course you will need a different adapter plug for each country. Even when you think you have them all, you will find some countries where your adapters won't work. Ask your hotel if they have adapters you can use. Before you travel abroad, purchase international modems or buy a computer already equipped with one.

Each country in Europe has different phone jacks, necessitating a variety of phone and electricity adapters. If the phone's jack doesn't plug in you can use acoustic couplers which will cradle the phone receiver and transmit the signals over speakers instead of through wires. Call Fax TeleAdapt at 408 370-5110 to purchase couplers and jack converters for a variety of international telephone plugs.

By the way, keep an international attorney's phone number handy in case someone sees you with all this high-tech equipment and arrests you as a spy or foreign agent. Many countries prohibit technology that bypasses their telecommunication equipment, but being a good salesperson we know you can talk your way out of it.

In Japan, dial tones are different. American modems don't recognize them. However, the appropriate Japan line can be added to the modem script in computers. At Radio Shack you can purchase a pocket tone dialer for about $20 that's about the size of a standard audiocassette. Program in your phone and credit card numbers, hold it up to the phone's mouthpiece, tell the memory what number you want, and the dialer will replicate the sound of a Touch-Tone phone and the call will go through.

Sprint offers Global Calling, Sprint Express, and a World-Traveler Foncard with English-speaking operators so you don't have to use a foreign operator when you travel. A WorldTraveler access code allows you to call from country to country, within the same country, or to the United States.

If you have gone through the hassle of hurdling the language barrier and trying to find the right foreign currency to use a pay phone, you will never again leave the country without this card or a similar one offered by other companies. You'll avoid trying to understand difficult dialing patterns in each country, surcharges for calling from hotels, and the hassle of trying to convert currency values. If you speak Japanese or Spanish, special cards and numbers are available from Sprint that link you with a customer service representative who speaks your language. Don't wait until you get there to try to arrange it. Set it up before you go and you'll avoid a tremendous amount of aggravation.

Padding the ol' expense account?

Everybody knows those business trips weren't all business and, hopefully, included a little monkey business. The trick is in making it all look legitimate to your company and IRS.

Use your Personal Data Assistant to keep track of your travel expenses, then download them into your computer. Pocket Quicken, a personal finance software, works with Radio Shack's Zoomer. *Money* magazine offers "Business Forms," which works with the Apple Newton.

If you work for Avery Dennison, a maker of office products in Concord Township, Ohio, you don't have the hassles of filling out traditional expense reports when you take a business trip. You simply call a certain "800" number and, guided by a computer voice response unit, use the phone's Touch-Tone keypad to key in the appropriate codes and dollar amounts corresponding to your expenses. Three days later, your bank account is credited with the amounts.

Avery Dennison uses Traveletter Direct Service which reimburses employees through direct deposit, automatically pays bills for corporate-sponsored credit cards, and provides detailed reporting to the company. The service, provided by Gelco PayNetwork of Edina, Minnesota, costs $2 to $4 per report. Companies are still responsible for matching employee receipts with the reports.

Given that Avery Dennison used to spend $8 to $10 per paper expense report, Patrick Curby, manager of accounting services, is quite pleased with the service. "It saves money, and it keeps the field people happy, since they can submit expense reports from wherever they are and get reimbursed quickly," he says.[4]

Bypass Baghdad Betty

And in case you're really worried about Bart Simpson making love to your wife while you're away, USAir and American Airlines have a service whereby you can send flowers to her from the plane. Or else call 800 FLOWERS or FTD at 800 253-0100. Maybe you'll even find a way to put them on your expense account.

Chapter 15

Get the Picture?
(Videoconferencing)

"Videoconferencing can put you out in front, wherever you may be. In sales, it's the next best thing to being there."
—David Topus[1]

You've heard it a million times before: "Get in front of the customer." Sitting in the office is unproductive, or so the theory goes; when you're in front of the customer you're selling. And now, thanks to advances in video communications technology, there's no excuse for not facing up to your customers.

Companies use videoconferencing for a host of purposes, from internal meetings to training sessions. In sales, where face-to-face interaction is critical, the technology opens a world of possibilities. Just take the case of Southern Pacific Railroad, which has videoconferencing capabilities in all seven of its regional sales offices.

When summer floods in the Midwest threatened Southern Pacific's service, the railroad called an emergency conference. "We were able to have a meeting right on the spot that would have been difficult, if not impossible, to have in person," says Peter Ruotsi, vice president of sales.

Even in less urgent situations, videoconferencing is "a salvation," says Ruotsi. Recently SP wanted clarification on a bid request from one of its customers, a large paper company in the

189

Northwest. Ruotsi patched in the customer in Portland with SP's Denver sales office and San Francisco headquarters.

"They were able to put the documents in front of us and describe line by line exactly what they wanted," he says. "Since we were able to see them face-to-face, we were in a better position to understand what they wanted and to respond."

SP also uses videoconferencing for strategy sessions, performance evaluations, and interviewing. But, he says, in-person meetings are still better "when things aren't happening the way they've been committed to or agreed to. When you walk into someone's office you can see much more of the total picture—more than what the camera wants you to see."[2]

Tony Visone, founder of the country's largest Corvette dealership, has a videoconferencing setup between his showrooms in Atlanta, Indianapolis, Los Angeles, Peabody, Massachusetts, Pompano, Florida, and his bank. When a shopper applies for financing at a given showroom, he or she is immediately introduced to a loan officer on-screen and is engaged in a tête-à-tête interview then and there. "A customer who sees the lender at inception causes fewer collection problems than one who never meets the lender," Visone notes. Another time and money saver: the thirty-one-year-old founder now travels less, "inspecting" each showroom via television every morning.[3]

The Electric Power Research Institute (EPRI) based in Palo Alto, California wanted to integrate their extensive collection of information and corporate training videos with their PictureTel videoconferencing system so they could be viewed on demand anywhere in the world. Ikonic Interactive in San Francisco digitized the videos from standard format tapes provided by EPRI and stored them to high-capacity disk drives. This created a prototype digital video database available worldwide for searching and viewing in real time via dial-up access on teleconferencing units by PictureTel.[4]

Videoconferencing is poised for explosive growth, as refinements in technology and reductions in costs have made it a widely accessible communications tool. According to the North American Telecommunication Association, videoconferencing was a $1.3-billion industry in 1993 and is expected to reach $6.9 billion in three years.

In the past, videoconferencing did not provide high quality sound or pictures and was considered a glorified conference call. Delayed response in signals made the picture jittery and conversation jerky. It was easy to miss visual cues and nonverbal cues.

Thanks to new technology in long-distance phone lines, videoconferencing links, television monitors, remote-control cameras, and digital transmission, the videoconferencing business is booming. Fiberoptics has improved the quality and lowered the price.

If you object to spending too much time and money on the road meeting with clients, attending sales meetings, watching hidden camera commercials being shot, or listening to focus groups behind a one-way mirror, you will want to check out the latest technology. Becoming video-ready is as easy as plugging the cord into the wall. The only hitch is having phone lines that can carry the extra-wide band width of video transmission (a nonissue once transmission can be carried over standard phone lines).

Not only does videoconferencing cut travel time and costs, but it allows more people to participate in the process. Remote control cameras allow observers to focus on a close-up of a particular individual or pan the entire group. A two-way sound system picks up what is being said and allows the observers to communicate with the moderator through an earpiece.

How to get the most from videoconferencing

David Topus, president of Topus & Associates, a Longmont, Colorado, sales-communication consulting and training firm, offers these guidelines:

Preparation

With videoconferencing, you're working with a new set of variables, so plan ahead. Make sure you:

- Write and distribute an agenda ahead of time
- Appoint a leader for each site and coordinate the connection times for each one in advance
- Practice using computer information and graphics on the camera

- Know where the fax machine is; better yet, have one right in the conference room
- Print materials in 14-point type or larger (put the document on the floor and make sure you can read it from a standing position)
- Check camera presets and practice changing camera angles

Presentation

- Introduce everyone in the room
- Speak in a normal volume
- Keep enough distance from the camera so that you don't block anyone's view
- Wear a medium blue or pastel shirt (no white!) with a solid, dark jacket
- Avoid clothing with any kind of highly detailed patterns
- Avoid bright, flashy jewelry that can reflect light

How much does it cost?

Videoconferencing, long a staple of science fiction's view of the twenty-first century, has made its way into only the most technologically-minded large companies. The reasons are simple: If you want to set up a meeting between, say, two groups of six people, you have to lay out more than $80,000 per video-conference room. And transmitting the signals between conferees by special connections such as fiber-optic phone lines or by satellite runs up a tab of $60 to $700 per hour.

But if videoconferencing rigs are expensive, so, too, are the alternatives. With rising air fares and hotel rates, a video-conference setup can justify its price tag fairly quickly by reducing or eliminating travel to meetings. And unlike telephone-conference calls, videoconferences allow you to see the expressions of those you're talking with, and everyone can share visual aids such as charts and graphs.[5]

The benefits are obvious, for large and small businesses alike. And it looks as though some day soon videoconferencing could be accessible to both. Smaller setups are already available.

For about $2,000 you can turn your personal computer into a personal videoconferencing system. The "personal" system is ideal for individuals because it works off a PC and is affordable. But the small screen makes it inappropriate for large meetings. For that, you'll need a system that will run anywhere from $14,000 to $28,000. Standard equipment includes a 20- or 25-inch monitor, a camera, a microphone, and a keypad—nothing that can't be found at an electronics store. The magic (and the cost), however, is in the software.

If you use a lot of charts, a special document camera can show the graphics on a screen next to the one the meeting is on (cost: approximately $2,500). For larger rooms with complex seating arrangements, a camera can be programmed to shoot from various angles (cost: about $2,000). And when key people scattered around the world need to be in on the meeting, a multiport capability enables you to bring them together (cost: from $39,000 to $90,000 and up, depending on the number of users).

If you don't want to buy your own equipment, contact Focus Vision Network of New York. They provide videoconferencing equipment and services in nine facilities throughout the United States. Their clients include advertising agencies and major corporations such as Apple Computer, AT&T, Levi Strauss, and Nabisco Foods. Transmitting a focus group costs around $1500 per session, or the equipment can be leased for between $3,500 and $5,000 a month.[6]

How to tune in and turn on

Here is your guide to videoconferencing vendors and their products.

The leading players in the field—PictureTel, Compression Labs Inc. (CLI), VTel, and GPT Video Systems—offer a full complement of equipment. Others have gotten into the act as well, including such electronics giants as Sony, Hitachi, Toshiba, and value-added resellers such as MCI, Sprint, and the Baby Bells. AT&T is also a major vendor of videoconferencing hardware and the long-distance network that supports it.

Together, these vendors will do everything from putting videoconferencing capabilities on your PC to creating a class-room-type setting with oversized video monitors and stereo-quality sound. Prices range from $6,000 for PictureTel's personal-sized series 100 (which runs on PCs) to $80,000 for VTel's Benchmark series, which includes two 35-inch monitors and features transmission times that are faster than a speeding sales pitch.

PictureTel Corp., which has been selling $14,000 to $40,000 corporate videoconferencing room systems for several years, is just rolling out a more affordable, ($6,000 to $58,000) add-on videoconferencing product for PCs running Microsoft Windows 3.1. The low-end PictureTel Live runs on a PC and offers video-windowing and speakerphone. The PCS 100 comprises two boards that provide the necessary video and audio compression for videoconferencing as well as Super VGA accelerated graph-ics, video-windowing for sharing, and an ISDN interface. Users must be connected to a public-switch digital network to provide the data link with other PictureTel Corp. videoconferencing systems, or any other digital videoconferencing system that adheres to international standards. Initial applications for the PC-based PictureTel include distance learning, telemedicine and telemarketing where visual communications are used in conjunc-tion with computing capabilities.[7] For more information call PictureTel at 800 716-6000 or 508 762-5000.

Sony is developing a camera/microphone/speaker module for desktop computers that will work with digital compression circuitry and network systems from other companies to create PC-based videoconferencing, according to Leo Flotron, Sony's marketing manager for videoconferencing.

Twincom brings you C-Phone for $1,995 per PC for desktop videoconferencing. Participants "meet" via their PCs to minimize time and location conflicts. C-Phone is an inexpensive PC-to-PC videophone system that delivers real-time, full-motion color video and synchronized audio from one desktop to another. You can use the system either on a network within your office or at a remote site (by using high-speed phone lines). The C-Phone system, which can support as many as 32 simultaneous two-way calls on either the Novell or Artisoft networks, comes with everything necessary for real-time desktop videoconferencing, a camera-microphone-speaker unit that sits atop the monitor, and all of the necessary software.[8]

Pro Share Personal Conferencing products range from a $100 Windows software program allowing users to share files over standard phone lines to a full videoconferencing system that costs around $2,000.

Hitachi's CA-200 system (404 446-8820) is a desktop system that includes a 10-inch monitor, a zoom camera, and a control unit. It sells for about $14,900 per station. The system can't handle large groups, but it can be very effective for one-on-one meetings.

The Cameo Personal Video System is a two-way interactive video system from Compression Labs ($2,095 to $4,195 per site, 800 538-7542). Two callers can see each other in a window on the screen of their Macintosh computers.

CLI. 800 538-7542. Three eclipse models, from $14,900 to $27,900. The low-end model has a 20-inch monitor and features auto focus and echo cancellation.

VTEL. 800 856-8835. Three systems ranging from $14,950 to $80,000. The low-end DeskMax has a 14-inch monitor and features electronic pan/tilt/zoom.

GPT video systems. 404 263-4781. Four systems ranging from $26,000 to $58,000. The low-end Focus 305 offers desktop dialing and picture-in-picture capabilities.

Several trends should soon give a major boost to videoconferencing, making it a viable option for some small businesses. As fiber-optic lines are brought to more homes and offices for uses such as improving telecommunications quality, the price of transmitting the large quantities of data required for video-conferences should drop significantly. And in the not-too-distant future, the equipment necessary to play back videotapes will likely become a standard feature in PCs, increasing the demand for videoconferencing and dramatically reducing its cost.[9]

Part IV

Layman's Guide for New Technologies
(Equipping the Virtual Office)

Chapter 16

Heard Anything Yet?
(Pagers)

"Nothing focuses the mind better than the constant sight of a competitor who wants to wipe you off the map."
—Wayne Calloway
CEO of PepsiCo

Brad Austin, a partner in Wallace & Company, a real estate firm on Martha's Vineyard in Massachusetts, was awaiting word from a prospective buyer of a waterfront house. The call never came—or so he thought. The next day, only an hour after the house was sold by another company, Austin learned that his client had, in fact, called to make an offer. Because the handwritten message had never made its way to Austin's desk, he'd lost a $375,000 sale.

"Needless to say, I wanted to kneecap my colleague," says Austin. Reason prevailed, though, and Wallace & Company installed a new communications system designed to prevent such mishaps. Handwritten phone messages are still taken, but now they're supplemented with messages sent directly to agents in the field by means of rented pagers, which scroll the information on their small screens. The person who takes the message simply types it into a stand-alone pager unit in the office, then issues a command to transmit it to the appropriate realtor. The pagers themselves are the same size as voice pagers and can store more than a dozen messages, just in case you need to refer back to an earlier one. The whole systems costs the company about $145 per month.

"We know we're saving time and money. And even more important, we have peace of mind, knowing that we're not missing important messages anymore," says Austin.

There's much more telecommunications technology available to Austin and his eight-member staff. They could, for instance, run their messaging system through software in their computers rather than through the stand-alone unit. "There are some great things out there that we haven't yet taken advantage of just because no one in the company is paid to take the time to learn about them and get things set up," says Austin.[1]

Pagers and palmtops

When is a messaging pager more than just a messaging pager? When it's linked directly to your computer network. With Notify!, a $149 software program from Ex Machina (800 238-4738), you can enter messages on preset forms you call up on your computer, then send them via modem through a paging-network service such as Air Signal, 800 821-5430, or Mobile-Comm, 800 685-5555—or satellite-transmission service such as SkyTel System, 800 456-3333, or Motorola's EMBARC, 800 EMBARC4—directly to pagers that display words or to palmtop computers. The program is available for DOS, Windows, and Macintosh systems.

Jon Corippo, operations manager of Valley Air Conditioning & Repair, in Fresno, California, says Notify! rescued his company from a dispatcher's recurring nightmare. His technicians had to call in repeatedly to check the addresses for their service assignments because their voice-pager messages were garbled or being drowned out by the roar of a passing truck. Now, instead of relying on voice pagers, Corippo and his dispatchers use Notify! to keep in touch with the company's force of twenty technicians, who cover a 350-mile territory extending from Modesto to Bakersfield.

"It's a godsend for us," says Corippo. "We use it like an electronic notepad, sending detailed information on service calls

200

throughout the day." The Notify! system is totally integrated with the office's database, says Corippo. "So when the dispatcher feeds information about a service call into the database, all he or she has to do is hit a command and the data is automatically pasted into the Notify! system. Hit one button on Notify!, and the service information is sent to the technician in the field, who receives it on a scrolling pager."

The money saved from fewer errors has far outstripped the system's cost. We're getting messages to our technicians more quickly now, and we're spending less time straightening out mistakes," Corippo says.[2]

How about you? Are you ready for beeps, buzzes, or vibrations in the night that send messages to your business pager, lifestyle pager, wristwatch pager, personal digital assistant (PDA), Newton MessagePad, laptop, and notebook computer? Ready or not, they're here. Millions of people use them and your customers know they can get a message to you within 120 seconds.

You're in sales. You need to know. *Now.* So check your beeper. Why do you need a pager? Various surveys reveal that approximately 88 percent of business phone calls don't get through to the desired parties. According to Message Processing Systems, the reasons phone calls don't get through are: 37 percent are out of the office; 18 percent are already on the phone; 14 percent are in a meeting; 13 percent don't want to be interrupted; 12 percent are at their desks but apparently don't feel like dealing with the phone; 6 percent are either hiding in the supply closet, in the rest room, or standing by the water cooler.[3]

How many of those lost calls represent lost sales for you? If you don't have a good answering system that you check regularly or voice mail, and are out of the office a lot, consider a pager.

Experts say the alphanumeric pager, an alternative to bulky, expensive cellular phones (and phone tag frustration), is headed for explosive popularity. Numeric paging has been around for a decade, but the new alphanumeric variety, which delivers text as well as numbers, is taking giant steps. According to surveys from Economic and Management Consultants International Inc. (EMCI) of Washington, D.C., 15.3 million pagers were in use in 1992, 30 percent more than the year before. Five percent of them were alphanumeric, up 60 percent from 1991. This year the number of alphanumeric pagers in use should hit 1.3 million, which would be about 7 percent of the total.

Numeric pagers

Dialer calls an access number, enters the PIN of the person he wants to reach, enters his phone number, then hits #. Pager will beep or vibrate to notify you of a call and record the number of the person who called.

NEC's Sport stores sixteen messages and sells for around $100. Their Business Card model is credit card–size and sells for $299.

Motorola offers Freespirit for $129. The Bravo Express sells for $169 and will time-stamp pages and retain memory when unit is off.

A variety of snazzy colors and designs are available and can be rented from paging services or purchased for between $100 and $300 from stores such as Target, Circuit City, and Macy's. Two basic types are available, but decide on your paging network service before you buy a pager.

Alphanumeric pagers

An alphanumeric pager works like a tiny radio, with a crystal inside. But unlike a radio, it listens only for its own messages, identified by what is called a "cap code." Once the pager receives a message, a computer chip decodes the information and puts words on the screen. It's the words that delight. "People prefer to get total information. They need to know, up to the minute, what's happening," says Julie Greene, Motorola marketing services manager in Boynton Beach, Florida. That means current—*really* current—prices can come in, silently, during a sales presentation. Or a real estate agent can receive the buyer's latest offer while meeting with the seller. The beep and wiggle don't just tap, they deliver.

Motorola products, such as the Advisor, represented 57 percent of the alphanumeric pager market in 1992, followed by NEC, with products such as the Provider, at 39 percent. Four-line, 80-character displays are common on top-of-the-line models, which can store up to forty messages each. The Advisor also has a clock, an alarm, a time-and-message stamp, user-selected alerts (pick how loud and how long), and a personal message file to store information. (Cheaper models erase messages when the pager turns off.) It has four code capabilities, which means it can receive individual messages, group messages (sales manager calling all reps), and information services. Oh yes: Sports scores, stock quotes, headlines, gambling aids (SportsPage from Beepers Plus, Las Vegas), etc. are available via pagers.

Pagers are light (NEC's Provider weighs only 3.4 ounces), bright (they come in colors like "sizzling yellow" and "vibra pink"), and can be read (at least some of them) from a belt, upside down. They use batteries, usually standard AAA or AA varieties that provide up to nine hundred hours of use. They are skinny (Motorola's Advisor, at 3.3-by-2.3-by-.08 inches, is the size of a credit card). Just so you know, some high schools outlaw pagers (and their faux brethren) because they're a drug-trafficking mainstay.

Alphanumeric pagers, which generally run $250 or more (Motorola's Advisor lists at $349), are rarely retail items, says Dan Blanton, product planner for Motorola's alphanumeric products. Most users lease pagers through paging or answering services; once again, service is king. The total cost averages $30 to $50 per month (compared with $10 to $25 for numeric devices), although it varies according to area. In Minneapolis, says Jerry Ramlet, sales manager for Airsignal (a division of McCaw Cellular Communications), $25 per month is the norm. Airsignal provides 300 messages at 230 characters per message for that cost; a deluxe service package includes 500 calls for $122.

Most alphanumeric messages are delivered the old-fashioned way: Someone answers the phone, takes the message, types it in (Motorola makes a transmission keyboard called AlphaMate), and sends it off. But you can do it with a computer and modem. Using dedicated systems or PC software, a desktop computer can transcribe its own alphanumeric messages, then relay them to a broadcaster over a modem. (Fourth Wave Technologies makes WinBEEP, a $129 software product; Ex Machina makes the similar Notify; Canamex Communications offer Quickpager for $549; Radio Technology makes AlphaPage for $139; Metriplex makes

PcPage and McPage for $249). You transmit to a carrier service; PageNet was the U.S. service leader in 1992, with over two million subscribers and a 62 percent growth rate from 1991. The nationwide paging leader was SkyTel, with 218,000 subscribers. According to EMCI, only 2 percent of customers subscribe to nationwide paging; 34 percent of service firms offer it.

SkyWord by Skytel stores messages of up to 240 characters and displays them 80 at a time on its LCD screen. Monthly leasing fee of $99 covers 50 alphabetic and 50 numeric incoming messages. For $10 per month customers may receive financial quotes twice a day on up to four companies. Limited two-way messaging technology is also available and will be expanded soon.

Before you sign up, check out the networks for quality, reliability, and price. Rates are far less than cellular service and range from $8 to $100 a month depending on the service and type of pager.

Alphanumeric pages are more expensive because a human operator is involved unless you send messages from a laptop with a radio modem. Local, regional, and national services are available for on the ground or in the air. MobileComm transmits in all fifty states plus the Virgin Islands and Puerto Rico. For more information, contact Paging Services Council at 202 333-0700.

Pagers keep communication short, sweet, and economical. They may well be the sales tool of the '90s. As communications technologies continue to merge, look for more in your beeper. Two-way communications are coming. In June the FCC designated three megahertz of the radio spectrum for wireless data communication and awarded an experimental "pioneer's preference" license to Mobile Telecommunications Technologies Corp. (Mtel) to develop its Nationwide Wireless Network. The system, operated via base stations and satellites, is expected to be in three hundred U.S. markets by 1995. It will link public and private E-mail systems, fax machines, voice-mail boxes, wireless devices like alphanumeric pagers—and you.[4]

Chapter 17

The Power of the Pen
(Personal Digital Assistants)

"Need a little help on the road? Say hello to your pint-sized Personal Digital Assistant."

—Cathy Madison[1]

There's much ado about very little in the hyperactive world of computing these days—a little something weighing less than one pound, or thereabouts. The technology prompting all the buzz is the Personal Digital Assistant, or PDA. The term Apple Computer coined (and acronym-addicted techies embraced) describes a new category of portable computing and communicating devices. Some people refer to them as personal electronic devices (PEDs).

It's the technology behind the PDA, not just its pint-sized package, that makes this new hybrid worth some study. PDAs combine the simplicity of pen and paper with the brainpower to manipulate information. They can help you work and communicate on the fly—calculate, take notes, add to your address book, update your calendar, write memos, fax messages. Some will help do accounting for you, manage your "out box," and even dial the phone. And, unlike a human assistant, it never calls in sick.

Companies like Sharp Electronics and Casio proved the need for small personal organizers, the predecessors to PDAs. But personal organizers do not include the most intriguing featu

PDAs tout—"intelligence," and the ability to assist a nontechnical consumer by using a pen, or "stylus," instead of a keyboard.

If you are a computerphobiac, you might want to break down the walls slowly by starting out with a simple PDA. But to be really useful, PDAs should be able to communicate. That means the notes, faxes, letters, and memos you create on the road should have a way to get out—either over wires (through phones, printers, or computer networks), or without wires at all (using infrared devices to transmit information to other PDAs or PCs up to six feet away).

Keep the "personal" part of Personal Digital Assistants in mind if you're in the market to buy one. Different makers have defined the mobile worker's needs differently. How much computing and communicating power do you need? How big and how heavy a PDA can you handle on the go? Do you prefer pocket-sized, handheld, or larger? How much money do you want to spend?

Salespeople will find many applications for a PDA in addition to its personal organization uses. The PDA's inventory capabilities would certainly make a car salesperson's job easier. Every day, or even two or three times a day, the PDA could be downloaded with an updated inventory list of every car on the lot. When a buyer arrives with certain specifications, a quick check on the PDA would tell the salesperson whether or not that exact vehicle is in inventory. If it's not in inventory, he could then take the necessary action needed to interest the prospect in alternative choices, or make arrangements to transfer the specified vehicle from another lot.

These amazing devices store handwriting as data and can be programmed to recognize your handwriting. If you teach your PDA that a circle is a G, then a circle is a G. If it doesn't recognize a word, it will save the word and type it exactly as it is written, misspellings and all. It will communicate with your PC, sending information such as business forms or expense reports to your PC and printer. Add a modem and it can reach the world.

PDAs are small and usually have no actual keyboard (some have keyboards that appear on the screen). The Newton Message-'ad from Apple ($699 list), for example, is the perfect size for grasping in one hand (and losing behind the seat or between the magazines, but we won't talk about that). Open the cover and you see a transparent tablet. Write on it. (Or, in these still-Dark Ages, print.) Some PDA models even recognize cursive. Memorization of the instructions is not necessary, because most PDAs include a self-help directory on the inside cover.

The PDA, using a low-power, inexpensive, and minute microprocessor, recognizes what you've written and translates it into text. Even more important is how it organizes data: It uses an object-oriented operating system that differs from a word-processing or spreadsheet program. Think of it as data soup —dump the ingredients in, and the PDA finds them, sorts them, and combines them any way you want.

Pen in your data and the PDA figures out what to do with it. Write a column of numbers and draw a line under it; the PDA gives you a total. Write in a lunch date with Natalie Cawood, and the PDA checks to verify which Natalie you're searching for, puts the date in your calendar, brings up her fax number so you can verify the date in writing, and gets the fax ready to send (in the form you prefer) next time you plug into a phone line. Erase something and the PDA knows what you mean. It also learns how you do things, so it can do them automatically for you in the future. Pretty Darned Aggressive, eh?

Since plans for these small hand-held computers hit the drawing board, manufacturers have promoted the new tool with promises of astonishing flexibility and friendliness: You can hold a PDA in your hand, slip it in your pocket, or hide it in your briefcase. You can have it zap a message to a colleague at the other end of the conference table, using wireless technology. You can scrawl on it with a pen, and it will read your writing. You can write "call Nathan Estruth," tap on it, and it will dial the number. You can write a memo, and tap, tap, it will automatically format the memo to your specifications and fax it off. You can stick in a little card and do a crossword puzzle, read a book, or see the latest headlines.

Just who, exactly, is going to use this thing? Cheap it ain't. PDAs range in price from $300 to $4,000. But never fear, says Gerry Purdy, vice president and chief analyst of mobile computing for Dataquest, a San Jose, California, computer analysis company: everybody you know will eventually have one. "Sometimes more than one," he says. "Sales force automation is a key vertical market application."

PDAs do what computers can't: manage personal information in a way that's easily portable; provide access to information that's particularly useful while roaming about (maps, restaurant guides, stock market reports); offer two-way messaging that will complement voice messaging at about one-tenth the cost. "Hey, it's 11:30. Where are you?" one PDA might beam to another. It's the wireless communication processing that Purdy thinks is most significant. But market penetration will take a while; he predicts only several hundred thousand PDAs will sell in 1995.[2]

Check out these PDAs

If you truly want to know all the who's and what's of the PDAs starting to pop up all over, start hoarding vacation time. Among the companies working on PDAs are Amstrad, Apple, AT&T, Atari, BellSouth, Casio, Compaq, Fujitsu, Hewlett Packard, IBM, Motorola, NEC, Sharp, Sony, Tandy, and Toshiba, to name a few. Both major and minor (make that lesser known, so far) software and hardware companies are racing to stake a claim in the market. Several big names are holding hands on these endeavors—a sure sign that they think the new technology is big stuff.

Some of the PDAs you can choose from are:

BellSouth/Simon have joined hands to bring you Simon, a PDA/cellular phone on which you can schedule appointments, make phone calls, and write notes. It looks like a cordless phone, weighs 18 ounces and includes wireless fax capabilities—all for around $899.

The Casio Z-7000, the result of a joint venture between Casio and Tandy (often called the "Zoomer" by its fans), combines a host of built-in applications, excellent communications capabilities, and ease of use to create a tool with outstanding versatility and portability. It's 1-by-4.2-by-6.8 inches and weighs 15.3 ounces. The Zoomer's $899 basic list price includes a calculator, world clock, dictionary, spelling checker and thesaurus, date book, to-do manager, free-form notebook, and sound capability. It works with character-oriented (clear, neat) printing. Plenty of miscellaneous features are available, even a "pocket" version of Intuit Inc.'s best-selling personal-finance program, Quicken. It stores printing as data, has a language translator, fits inside a coat pocket, and can share data with PCs. Add a modem and it communicates worldwide. Available at a Radio Shack near you.[3]

Hewlett Packard's HP 100LX palmtop PC includes a phone book and appointment book that shows week and month at a glance; access to your office E-mail systems; built-in MS-DOS 5.0, which means you can run optional PC software such as Quicken, Microsoft, Project Manager, and ACT. You can create custom databases and sort through a list of customer billing profiles; or bring up Lotus 1-2-3, Release 2.4, for your spreadsheets. Use it as a financial calculator and flexible phone book. Weighing in at 11 ounces, you can see it at your nearest Hewlett Packard dealer or call 800 443-1254, Dept. 989. It sells for around $749.

At $399, Scottsdale Technologies Amstrad PenPad PDA 600 is an affordable alternative. Measuring 6.25-by-3.5-by-1 inches and weighing just 14 ounces, the PenPad offers much of the same functionality as other PDA devices. The PenPad uses a pen to navigate through its programs, including an address book, appointment scheduler, "to do" list, and notepad. The handwriting recognition translates handwritten characters into typewritten characters and can be trained by the user to recognize his own style of writing. Optional programs include a spreadsheet, word processor, and translator. A communications program, currently in development, will work via a modem. Also in development is a joint venture between Bill Lacy of Time Systems in Chandler, Arizona and Scottsdale Technologies.

Sharp's Expert Pad is very similar to Apple's Newton PDA. It has handwriting recognition, but it takes a while to learn your individual handwriting style, especially if you write like some doctors. This PDA contains icons to help you navigate. However, you will need to spend a fair amount of time with the owner's manual before finding your way around with any degree of confidence. If you want to erase something, just scribble over it (unless you write like a doctor). To select text, just draw a line through it or circle it. To edit a word, just tap on the word you want edited. It also has the capability to schedule meetings and fax memos or notes.[4]

Accessorizing your PDA

EMBARC, by Motorola, unlocks the potential of your PDA with its wireless network. All you need is the EMBARC Motorola NewsCard wireless data receiver and a wealth of wireless news and information comes straight to your PDA. Wherever you are in the United States and Canada, it will bring you a broad array of subscription news and information services. Dozens of subject options from such leading sources as *USA Today, Reuters*, and *Individual, Inc.*, keep you up to speed with everything from financial market updates to industry-specific news to sports and weather. It also keeps track of the full-text wireless E-mail and file transfers from your office. The EMBARC Motorola NewsCard fits many popular PDAs including the Casio Z-7000 "Zoomer" and GRiD 2390. For $249 you can turn your PDA into a wireless wonder. Call 800 EMBARC4, Ext. 530.[5]

Hyped today, here tomorrow

Although critics say PDAs have been over hyped, and maybe they have to some extent, they are here to stay. While still a novelty to some people, they are beginning to replace traditional office equipment such as fax machines, appointment books, and, eventually, dictation equipment. The PDA of today, like the first light bulb of yesterday, has a few kinks, but will soon become an indispensable tool for salespeople on the go.[6]

Chapter 18

Honey, They Shrunk the Computer
(Notebook Computers)

"The computer business is changing so quickly these days that sometimes we feel as if we're in the fresh-produce business."
—Safi Qureshey, cofounder and CEO
AST Research, Irving, California

Remember when you bought your first car? Did you know everything about its internal operations, or were you more interested in "will it get me where I want to go, in style?" Well, the same basic rules apply to the purchase of your first portable computer. In other words, you don't need to know the difference between a microprocessor and a microorganism to get the most out of a portable computer. And, don't go into a computer store thinking the clerk will answer all questions to your satisfaction. A few stores are truly helpful, but many either staff technical wizards who might as well speak Greek and who make you feel technologically challenged, or minimum-wage clerks with little practical knowledge of computer usage for sales applications. Some stores are the exception, but don't rely on their expertise alone.

Make sure your notebook computer is compatible with your desktop computer at your home or office, and comfortable to use and carry. Size, weight, battery life, and screen visibility are key factors.

Honey, they shrunk the computer

Over $640 million worth of notebook computers were sold retail last year, according to Personal Technology Research. Twenty percent were used in home offices.

A salesperson on the go, whether in the car calling on customers or on the plane, needs a laptop or notebook computer, either of which runs on batteries for hours, yet has the performance of a desktop computer.

The smallest full-function portable computers, called notebooks, weigh between four and seven pounds, and are about the size of a three-ring binder.

Their battery life is two to four hours. Subnotebooks have full functionality and a full-sized keyboard. They weigh between two and four pounds and have a battery life of eight to ten hours without a charge.

The larger versions, laptops, have more power, expanded capabilities, and often are the size of a large briefcase, weighing as much as twenty pounds. Prices range from about $1,000 to over $10,000 for top-notch multimedia laptops, including color display screens.

If you select one with a color screen, you will find a tremendous price difference between a passive matrix and an active matrix color screen. Color monitors can not only do more, but they alleviate the eyestrain associated with less color. If you don't want to spend approximately $1300 more for active color, remember you can always purchase a color monitor for around $500 which will attach to your laptop when you are at home or in the office. Your eyes will thank you.

Making the decision of which portable computer to use is a time-consuming and sometimes expensive endeavor. The first step involves knowing what functions you need to streamline your operation, both now and in the future. After detailed requirements are defined, a closer estimate should be made of both the real and hidden costs of the computer.

Real costs, such as the actual equipment, software programs, and supplies are relatively simple to identify. Hidden costs include items necessary for the support of a system. One computer may have a low initial cost with a high maintenance cost; for another, the opposite may hold true. How long is the warranty? Can it be serviced locally? Is it upgradeable? Does it come with a carrying case? Extra batteries? A battery charger? A modem? What software, if any, is included in the basic price? What other special features does it have? Some computers are expensive to hook up, or "dock," to the main computer and other peripherals in your office. Make sure your laptop is compatible with your desktop computer. Some laptops slide into a port on your desk, connecting it to a full-size monitor and your network. Others can be connected by using adapters.

These variations must be compared. Each vendor's proposal should be examined until there is a well-founded understanding of all costs involved. Remember, the computer and software you choose should conform to you, not the other way around.

The bottom line—what's out there

Apple Powerbooks range from about $1800 to $3500 with color screens, 4MB expandable to 14MB, an internal drive floppy disk, and is compatible with MAC Windows or OS/2s and all the interface ports. Apple has a two-pound PowerBook with a credit-card size hard disk. Their 540c PowerBook weighs around seven pounds and has a battery life of three to six hours. Call 800 538-9696.

IBM's ThinkPad 500 weighs 3.8 pounds, including the battery. IBM ThinkPad 720C weighs 7.6 pounds and has a large color screen and a pointing device. An added feature is its removable hard-disk drive, which makes it possible to select and carry only the clients' records, history and presentation materials that you are going to use on a given day or week for sales calls, enabling you to leave your other data back at the office. If you have ever lost your computer or had a hard drive crash, you know the value of this feature. For more information call 800 772-2227.

The IBM ThinkPad 750C Multimedia System weighs 5.5 pounds and features a Traveling Multimedia option that delivers every element necessary for creating or presenting multimedia output at remote sites. The additions increase the weight to 11.7 pounds. It lists for $8,599. Call 800 IBM-2YOU or 800 426-2968.

Compaq has designed their durable, reliable notebooks with sophisticated power conservation tools in order to get longer use out of batteries, and they come with easy-to-read screens. Their 486SL has 4MB RAM which can be upgraded to 20MB and a 120MB or 209MB hard drive. It weighs in at 6.4 pounds. Their Contura Aero 4/25 weighs 3.5 pounds and has a battery life of six hours. Compaq claims their notebooks are like an armadillo with rugged engineering that makes them the most durable on earth. Apparently they withstand dropping, baking, and freezing, but hopefully your sales territory won't take you to those extremes unless your business is selling Timex watches. For more information call 800 345-1518. Ask about the Concerto model, a powerful 33 MHz 486 convertible portable which handles either pen or keyboard input, has a screen that can stand upright when detached from the keyboard, and a handle that doubles as a display stand. Prices start at $2,499 and include InkWare NoteTaker and PenPower for the pen applications. Call 800 345-1518.

Zenith Data System's Z-Lite 425L is a 486SL notebook. Weighing in at less than four pounds, it starts at around $1,899.

NEC's new notebook, the Versa E Series, includes a screen that can be flipped around for presentations or used as a pen-based tablet. The pen can be used to make changes, update a presentation, or record a signature. It has brilliant graphics, monochrome or color, and ten hours of battery life. The $6,000 price includes high-capacity batteries, plus the option of replacing the floppy disk drive with an additional battery. Both the screen and hard drive can be replaced, allowing several people to use the same computer by inserting their own hard drive. Their DX4/75 weighs 6.6 pounds and has a battery life of three hours. Call 800 632-4636.

The GRiD Convertible 486 by AST Research Inc., accommodates pen as well as keyboard input, weighs 6 pounds and measures 2.1-by-11.6-by-9.6 inches. It sells for under $2,000. Call 800 876-4278.

Hewlett-Packard's OmniBook 300 (a subnotebook) weighs 2.9 pounds, runs DOS and Windows applications, comes with a pop-out mouse, an electronic phone book, a financial calculator, and will run ten hours on four AA batteries. It sells for around $1,600.

The Toshiba T1900C notebook computer with a color display screen made it possible to write this book in a variety of locations. Check out the Toshiba Portege T3400, a subnotebook weighing 4.1 pounds. The T3400CT weighs 5.4 pounds and has a battery life of three to six hours. Prices range from $1,699 for a T1900 black and white screen to $3,999 for the active-matrix color version. Call 800 334-3445.

Epson's ActionNote 700 weighs 4.4 pounds with a mono-chrome screen and 4.9 pounds with active-matrix color, and measures 8.6-by-11-by-1.4 inches. It sells for under $2,000 and features a removable hard drive. Call 800 289-3776.

The competition for the tiniest office heated up recently as Dauphin Technology, of Lombard, Illinois, began shipping the DTR-1, which claims title to the world's tiniest 486 computer. Its central processing unit, separate keyboard, six-inch mono-chrome screen, carrying case, and internal battery, collectively, weigh a mere 3.5 pounds. This lilliputian setup takes up only half a briefcase, but you can save even more space by jettisoning the keyboard in favor of an electronic stylus (supplied), which serves also as a mouse. Through preinstalled Windows for Pen Comput-ing, a user can teach the DTR-1's built-in spreadsheet to recog-nize even sloppy handwriting. Nirvana it's not; the characters must be in printed, rather than cursive, form.

Inside the DTR-1 is a silver-dollar-size hard disk, storing about 40 megabytes. A fax/modem is also built in, but, as with most pen-based systems, a floppy drive isn't. Instead, the DTR-1 can hook up to an external floppy or hard drive. Anyway, you can always download via cable from a desktop PC. But while you're there, hook up the machine to a keyboard and monitor that's fit for grownups. This miniature marvel may be a great traveling companion, but when you're back in your office, your eyes will let you know how they feel about it. The DTR-1 costs about $2,500. For information, call Dauphin at 800-782-7922.[1]

New kid on the dock

When you bring your laptop back to your home office and want to use a larger monitor to save your eyes and a standard size keyboard to relieve your hands, you can hook it up to one of several docking stations on the market, or you can plan in advance and buy a computer that fits into its own dock. Texas Instruments' Intelligent Docking Station is designed for TI's TravelMate laptop and fits into it just like a videotape into a VCR. The docking station automatically configures the laptop and it even charges the battery. Available for $895.

If you want to connect your PC to the mainframe, exchange files, and cut and paste data between your mainframe and your laptop, invest $425 in Attachmate Extra! for Windows.

IBM's ThinkPad 700C can be connected to a docking station. A Duo Dock System is available for Apple PowerBook users. The MiniDock is portable and makes it easy to hook into an external monitor.

Rules, rules, rules

You're prepared and you make good use of your time. During a long cross-country flight in first class, you intend to revise and customize your sales presentation for your next appointment. As soon as you get started, along comes the flight attendant and asks you to turn off your computer because it may interfere with aircraft systems.

But what about your rights as a frequent flyer, you ask. And what about your "to-do" list and schedule, for which you allotted three hours computer work time on the plane?

Laptop computers are indispensable for traveling salespeople, but don't expect to get a lot done on the airplane. Airlines request that all electronic devices be turned off during takeoff and landing, and many would like to see them prohibited while flying in the air at all.

And, don't run your laptop through the electronic security devices. Your magnetic software disks could be damaged. Instead, hand it to one of the attendants, who will then ask you to turn it on and prove it is a computer. If your battery is dead hopefully you didn't pack your power cords in your check-in luggage or you may have to make the trip alone while your computer waits with airport security.

Speaking of rules, did you know it is illegal to copy someone else's software? Most software programs are protected by copyright, just like books. The American Software Publishers Association takes this quite seriously. You are better off buying the programs from a reputable dealer, rather than taking a chance on a hefty fine, or even jail time.

Finally . . .

Still confused? If you need help in selecting the right computer for your applications, you can call 800 586-5504 and order *The 45-Minute Guide to Buying Your First Computer* or *Upgrading Your Old Computer* for $7.95. Also check with *What to Buy for Business* at 800 247-2185, or *The Office Equipment Advisor* by John Derrick, or other consumer publications. Subscribers to *Inc.* will find valuable information in special issues of *Inc. Technology*, published in March, June, September, and November.

The decision of which computer to purchase is similar to any other business decision. It requires step-by-step analysis of the situation, prioritization, confidence, and good judgement. Therefore, selecting a portable computer does not have to be a terrifying or disastrous experience. Knowledge helps to diminish fear, so rational decisions can be made. With a little education, you can triumph over these "mini-monsters" that are entrusted with so much vital information. And, if you are still confused about which laptop is best for you, buy one, hook it up, and ask it.

Chapter 19

Roll the Presses
(Portable Printers)

Customer to customer service rep at computer store, "I'd like to return this laptop printer . . . my cat is jealous of it."
— Cartoon caption

What to buy for business

Want to revise a document on the road? Pull out the portable printer.

When laptop and notebook computers began invading the briefcases of the mobile sales forces, portable printers couldn't have been far behind. But they are, says Steve Lapacz, an assistant vice president at Aid Association for Lutherans (AAL) in Appleton, Wisconsin. "It's one piece of technology that has not advanced as fast as the rest of the components." Yet AAL needs to print out new business applications for on-the-spot signatures, presentation materials, and the like, so it uses more than eighteen hundred of the technically cumbersome little devices. Although they are not as fast, light, and cheap as one might hope, new options are emerging for the expanding porta-computing market.

Before you make a decision on a portable printer, think about how you will be using it. Will you need it for color presentation charts? Printing or desktop publishing? Letters of agreement or sales contracts? Color transparencies for your presentations? Field correspondence and envelopes? For long or short documents? For all of the above or none of the above?

Some of the features to consider are type of paper or transparencies you will be using, whether or not you will need to print envelopes, and whether or not it is compatible with your laptop or notebook computer and/or your personal digital assistant (PDA). Will you need a parallel or serial computer port? Speed might be a factor if you will be printing in front of your customer as opposed to in your car or hotel room. Will the printer work in your car on the 110-volt adapter for your cigarette lighter? (The adapter is available for around $100.)

Keep in mind whether you want to word-process or publish. A Postscript printer handles fancy type and illustrations, but you may only need a font or two and a choice of printing modes: draft, fast, normal, best. The better the output, the slower the printer and the more battery and cartridge life you'll use. Speeds vary from three to six pages per minute.

Paper is easy. Most models use plain paper, although high-quality laser paper is best. Ditto for transparencies, which is the primary reason to tote a printer in the first place. If you need envelopes, better make sure the model you're considering handles them. Some printers use tractor feeds; others have trays. The Diconix 701 handles thirty sheets, and the MobileWriterPS holds up to eighty. Complaints about the ease of use, however, often center on tray attachment mechanisms.

You've heard it before, but really pay attention this time: make sure the model you love is compatible with your laptop and easy to use. Steve Lapacz of AAL says salespeople with live prospects should not have to mess around with cables and complicated hookups. In fact, his company based its choice of models partly on the fact that the user could simply open up a briefcase and have both computer and printer ready to roll. Compatibility also may cost you. The Diconix 701, for instance, needs a $79 power kit in order to hook up to a PowerBook. Also, different models are available for parallel or serial computer ports.

Ink is a financial as well as an aesthetic consideration. Some portable printers are ink-jet printers; others are the thermal fusion variety. Thermal fusion is considered higher quality, with 360 dots per inch (dpi) resolution in the WriteMove II, for example. The ribbons for thermal fusion printers are either single strike (high quality) or multistrike (for drafts) and cost $5 each. (Security experts note they also hold negative images of your documents, so be forewarned.) Ink-jet cartridges for the Mobile-WriterPS cost $15 but last for about 150 pages, which makes the cost per page about 10 cents. The WriteMove II costs 25 cents per page, according to trade magazine *Macweek*. Apple's new Portable Stylewriter milks 500 pages from its $20 cartridge, says Steve Gronau, a sales rep at First Tech in Minneapolis.

Portability, of course, is a relative term. Kodak makes the Diconix 701, which weighs 5.6 pounds, as well as the Diconix 180si, at 2.9 pounds. The MobileWriterPS from the Mannesmann Talley Corp., a near-laser-quality Postscript printer, is a hefty equal to the Macintosh PowerBook at 11.4-by-8.7-by-2.3 inches and 8.4 pounds (at least carrying one on each side will keep your arms at even lengths). GCC Technologies' WriteMove II is a more petite partner at 2 pounds and 11.5-by-3.5-by-2 inches. Don't forget to add the weight of batteries and a carrying case sturdy enough to handle all this technology.

The battery is always the stickler in portability. Check life, weight, cost, and recharge time. The nickel cadmium batteries used in the Diconix 180si last about fifty minutes (one hundred pages), recharge in about four hours, and can be found everywhere. The Diconix 701, on the other hand, needs a Sony Hi8 camcorder battery ($40) that lasts about the same time but takes ten to fourteen hours to recharge.

The portable printers discussed here list from about $329 for the low-end Diconix model to $999 for the only Postscript entry, the MobileWriterPS. Others are comfortably in the $400 to $600 range. As always with computer products, check mail-order catalogs and stores like Sears as well as higher-end computer stores.[2]

Also check out the Canon Portable Bubble Jet Printer—it's fast. It's also light—just 3.7 pounds. And it goes where you do. Available for under $250. Hewlett Packard offers a Portable Ink Jet Printer for $360.

And if a portable printer isn't in your budget, you can make a local phone call, use your fax modem, and fax the document to yourself at your hotel or the closest copy center. Other options include going to a secretarial service or copy center such as Kinko's or AlphaGraphics and hooking up to their printer. Some of the larger office equipment and products stores also offer this service. Call and ask for their incoming fax line number and for a small fee you can send and receive your faxes there. If you're in a rural area where these services aren't available, you can always ask your customer if your formats are compatible and if so, print out your sales proposal or contract on her printer. But you'd better be ready with an excuse for why you won't spring for a $300 printer.

Chapter 20

Everything You Need to Know to Pick (and Pack) a Portable Phone
(Cellular Phones)

"One irony of modern business communications is that the more ways there are for people to call you, the harder it is for them to reach you. Do they call your work phone, home phone, cellular phone, pager, or send a fax?"

—Betty Beard

How do I call thee? Let me reconcile the ways

AccessLine Technologies Inc. of Bellevue, Washington developed technology to simplify this problem of too many numbers to call, making separate home, office, fax, and pager numbers a thing of the past. Numbers will be assigned to people, not places. AccessLine allows customers to have one telephone number where they can be reached, including the office, car, home, or out of town.

According to Tim Samples, area general manager for US West Cellular, AccessLine is "like a remote control that consolidates the programming of a stereo, VCR, and television. It can control calls to a customer's home phone, office phone, fax machine, voice mail, cellular phone, and pager."

Callers will hear a computerized voice listing their options including leaving a message, transferring a call, or paging. It can be used to screen calls or give certain people a special number to reach you. It can also put callers on hold while you find a phone and get connected. Another feature includes transferring calls if you tend to be in the same place at the same time every day.

A penny for your call?

Talk is cheap, as the saying goes, but if you're planning on talking on a cellular phone, you might disagree. Once considered a luxury, cellular phones are now considered a necessity for every salesperson who sells outside of an office environment.

"Cellular" is a technology, not a service. It refers to transmission on radio frequencies, or channels, between cell sites, or cells. There are cells nearly everywhere in the United States where there's a highway or a metro or rural service area. In the population centers, you will have at least two licensed carriers to choose from. The service probably won't vary much, but the pricing plans will. A typical monthly fee might be $24.95; per-minute costs (some charge by the half-minute) usually run between 25 cents and 45 cents. You pay for time spent on the phone, regardless of who makes the call. According to the Cellular Telephone Industry Association (CTIA), the average monthly bill as of the end of 1992 was $68.68, down from $96.83 five years ago. One factor in average monthly costs is so-called "windshield time," or average commuting distance. Car people tend to have higher bills, so those who live in Los Angeles should be more careful than those who live in Des Moines, regardless of the basic cost.

The good, the bad, and the ugly?

In a 1993 survey by The Executive Committee in San Diego on the use of cellular phones, the top benefits were: keep people in constant contact (59.6 percent); increase productivity (56.4 percent); help sales and service (53.9 percent); valued as a perk

(16.4 percent); function as a modem/fax (1.8 percent); and emergency tool (1 percent).

However, the drawbacks mentioned were: have poor sound quality (27.1 percent); encourage too many personal calls (22.5 percent); make driving unsafe (12.1 percent); make billing too confusing (8.6 percent); make have-nots jealous (7.5 percent); increase car theft (6.8 percent).

Take your pick

The phones themselves come in three varieties: mobiles, or the old "car phones" (they cost about $140 to install, which you should keep in mind if you're about to buy a car); transportables, which are car phones made portable; and the popular portables, the self-contained one-piece units often called pocket phones. Between 70 and 80 percent of all cellulars in use fit into the latter two categories.

Mobile

A mobile phone is permanently installed in your car, the Transceiver in your trunk, and the handset inside, some with hands-free operation. Positioned so they are easy to use, they won't fly off their holder when you slam on the brakes. Their maximum allowable power is three watts but most provide good reception.

If possible, have it installed at the factory when you order your car. If the installation company is not familiar with the electrical system on the car it can cause unlimited problems since mobile phones draw power from the car's electrical system.

Portable

Much smaller in size and lighter in weight, with a maximum weight of 26 ounces, portables are easy to carry and operate. Due to their small battery packs they have a limited talk time. They're generally more difficult to use while you drive due to smaller keypad, no hands-free use, and with 0.6 watts of power are limited in range and quality. Pull over to the curb when you use this phone or use it when you aren't driving.

Transportable

Weighing up to eight pounds, with their battery packs, places restrictions on the word "transportable." It plugs into your cigarette lighter, operates on three watts of power, and doesn't affect the car's electrical system. However, you may only have two hours of talk time without recharging or changing batteries.

While all the above-mentioned phones use analog electronics, they will soon be replaced with digital cellular telephones. You will still be able to use your existing phone, but the digital phones will have many advantages in that they will have less distortion, higher security, no limit to subscribers, and will be able to send computer information without a modem.

Which to buy?

The key to deciding which phone to buy depends on how much you will use it and where you will use it most—in the car or on the run. There are more than sixty models of portable phones on the market, and prices run from about $100 to $2,200. The lighter the weight, the heavier the expense. Weights range from 5.9 ounces (for the Motorola MicroTAC Ultra Light) to 18.6 ounces (for the Motorola Ultra Classic and the Pioneer PCH-600, both of which have 132 minutes of talk time and 30 hours of standby time). Beyond that, the difference between models is like the difference between a Rolls Royce and a Yugo.

If you'll only be using the phone when your car breaks down or you're late for dinner, it won't matter if it rattles a lot. But if you use it for business, you can't afford to miss a call. Buy the best you can manage, and make sure you deal with a reputable retailer. You might also check with your service provider (there are two licensed in each area, and by regulation, one is the area's Baby Bell). Some give away phones as parts of promotions. Also, look for a digital-compatible phone, even though it costs a little more. Today's cellular technology is analog, but tomorrow's will be digital. The Fujitsu PCX contains a pager function, a voice chip that tells callers to dial in their phone numbers if you don't answer.

When you're shopping look for:

- a lighted keypad
- display screen large enough to show the entire number you're calling
- volume control for conversing in heavy traffic or noisy, crowded places
- large buttons for easy, accurate dialing of smaller models
- rapid battery charger
- additional battery pack
- car adapter with antenna to save your battery and give you hands-free speaking capability (which is required by law in some states)
- pager capability
- leather carrying case for added protection[1]

A-roaming you may go, but it will cost you. The approximately eleven hundred U.S. cellular phone companies have reciprocal agreements for those who leave home and take their phones with them. The "roaming" charge averages $2 to $3 a day, plus 95 cents a minute. Call delivery services, such as Follow Me Roaming (offered by GTE Telecommunication Services) or RoamingAmerica, automatically forward your calls to wherever you might happen to be. They offer other features and some limitations (when roaming, you can't use custom-calling features). Check your local carrier for the service available in your area.

There are bells and whistles features that salespeople, especially those who work in their cars, would do well to consider. The hand-free operation feature works like an office speakerphone. Hands-free answering automatically picks up incoming calls. Most portable phones can store names and numbers. Some have "call-in-absence" indicators, which inform users about calls that came in while they were away (optional horn-alert systems will beep the car horn when a call comes in). And some cutting-edge models even boast voice-activated dialing.

If you want to be the first on your force with the latest in phone technology, fish $1,295 out of your pocket and lay it down for the Fujitsu PCX. It measures a mere 5.4-by-2.3 inches, is less than an inch thick, and weighs just 7.4 ounces. Blaupunkt's TC 153 cellular phone only weighs 6.9 ounces and costs around $500. Its rounded design makes it easy to slip into your pocket. A sliding door keeps buttons hidden when not in use. Motorola offers a phone for $239 that weighs 6.9 ounces and fits in the palm of the hand.

Batteries are something that should be considered when purchasing any type of on-the-road phone, because they're all different.

If your phone is in your pocket, you're still in the minority. But that minority is getting bigger. According to the CTIA, by the end of 1992 the US had 11 million cellular users, compared with a bit more than 7.5 million at the end of 1991. Some 9,500 new subscribers are being added daily. If you compare the rate of cellular growth with the rate of growth for telephones, it's roughly five to one. Experts estimate that by the year 2000, this country will have reached its saturation point with cellular phones, and that means about 90 percent to 95 percent of American adults will have them.

Paranoid about your privacy? You should be. Listening in on cellular calls is illegal, thanks to the Electronic Communications Privacy Act of 1986. But those who scan frequencies as a hobby are rarely caught and are still pleasantly occupied. Security systems are available, although they can cost as much as several thousand dollars.

Security systems come in two varieties: those that scramble the airwave signals (they're less expensive but require special equipment operated by local carriers) and what are called end-to-end encryption systems. The latter are pricey and use matching scramblers, so both the caller and the receiver need to have one. Scanning will be more difficult when digital cellular technology becomes standard, but until then, you'll either have to spend the extra dollars or assume you're Princess Di and everybody is listening.[2]

Cellular voice messaging

When you don't answer your phone you can have the calls forwarded to the message center or to another number. If your messages are not forwarded to the message center and you want to retrieve messages, contact your subscribing service to get the system access number for the city you are in. If you use a cellular phone take advantage of its message center, but check your messages on a regular basis.

A very common complaint we hear all the time is that people leave a message at the message center and the salesperson may not check it for a few days or a week. Keep your message center–alert pager with you in your briefcase so you will be notified of a message by a flashing light or audio tone. You can always put it on "do not disturb" when you are with a client.

Is there a car phone in your future?

A survey by PacTel Cellular revealed that small businesses tend to be more generous with cellular phones than large ones. Companies with twenty to ninety-nine employees provide 14 percent of their workers with cellular telephones. Companies with more than one thousand employees provide phones for only 8 percent. Fifteen percent of small companies limit their cellular phone privileges to business hours while only 8 percent of the larger companies do. Among both large and small companies, 90 percent of the CEOs have cellular phones.[3]

Another survey by *Inc.* magazine revealed that 25 percent of the respondents felt their cellular phones were indispensable, 32 percent felt they were worthwhile, 28 percent said they can't live without them, and 12 percent do not use cellular phones.[4]

Afterword
(High-Tech vs. High-Touch)

"His phone is busy, his mailbox is busy, his fax is busy, and his modem is busy. I'll just walk over and talk to him."

Cartoon caption by Sidney Harris[1]

The true winners in sales will be the ones who figure out a way to use technology but keep the personal touch. This is possible by using high-tech for high-touch.

As society becomes more reliant on machines, it's imperative we use available technology to store as much information as possible about our customers so we can add a personal touch to our communications.

How you do it will depend on your target and whether or not that personal touch is a one-on-one face-to-face communication or through some form of technology. A personal touch doesn't have to be in person, but it must show that you know enough about your current customer so they feel you know and care about them personally.

Don't go overboard with technology and forget about individual clients. Use different mediums to reach them, but keep the focus on the customer. Some clients readily accept new technology, while others resist it. Be as flexible as possible without slowing down your progress.

Technology not only changes our sales techniques, but also forces changes in attitudes. Here are some of the differences we see in attitudes and selling techniques from the past and how technology has changed them:

Old	New
Establish rapport	Establish long-term relationships
Build your business	Build their business
Talk	Listen
Message	Medium
Persuasion	Need assessment techniques
Tell them about your product	Information agent
Work on your problems	Solve their problems
Market share	Share of customer
Push what you have	Help them find what they need
Local market	Global market
Every man for himself	Strategic partnerships
The salesmen in *The Tin Man* movie	Integrity selling
How the salesmen in the Glengarry Glen Ross movie obtained leads	CD-ROM prospecting on databases
Close sale	No "sales"—just ongoing relationships

We leave you with a quote from Leon Leonwood Bean (1872-1967), founder of the L.L. Bean outdoor-clothing company, "No sale is really complete until the product is worn out, and the customer is satisfied."

Footnotes

Chapter 1:   Will Your Company or Career Be Uprooted by the Forces Of Technology?

1.   Daniel Burrus, *TechnoTrends*. New York: HarperBusiness, 1993, p. 279.
2.   Gary Samuels, "CD-ROM's First Big Victim," *Forbes,* February 2, 1994, p. 42. Reprinted By Permission of *Forbes* Magazine copyright Forbes Inc., 1994.
3.   Joel Arthur Barker, *Paradigms,* New York: HarperBusiness, 1992, p. 17.
4.   Michael Hammer and James Champey, *Reengineering the Corporation,* New York: HarperBusiness, 1993, p. 23.
5.   Ibid.
6.   *Wall Street Journal* ad, February 14, 1994, p. A12; phone interview with marketing director, personal experience with the service; and Jay Finegan, "Sing to Me, Baby," *Inc.,* August 1993, pp. 90-98. Reprinted with permission, *Inc.* magazine, August 1993. Copyright 1993 by Goldhirsh Group, Inc., 38 Commercial Wharf, Boston, MA 02110.
7.   Daniel Akst, "In the Information Age, Everyone's a Revolutionary," *Los Angeles Times,* The Cutting Edge, April 11, 1994, p. 5.
8.   Thomas Forbes, "How to Get Up to Speed on the Selling Superhighway," *Selling,* May 1994, p. 49. Reprinted with permission.
9.   George Colombo, *Sales Force Automation,* New York: McGraw-Hill, 1994, p. 17.
10. Alice LaPlante, "It's Wired Willy Loman," *Forbes ASAP,* Spring 1994, p. 49. Reprinted By Permission of *Forbes* Magazine copyright Forbes Inc., 1994.
11. Andy Kessler, "Fire Your Sales Force--Empower Your Customer ," *Forbes ASAP,* February 28, 1994, p. 29. Reprinted By Permission of *Forbes* Magazine copyright Forbes Inc., 1994.
12. "Who's Blue?" Paul B. Carroll, *Selling,* August 1993, p. 52. Reprinted with permission.
13. Jane Bryant Quinn, "WIN Makes Middleman the Loser," *Scottsdale Progress Tribune,* March 1, 1994, p. C6.
14. Paul Gibson, "Five Ways Computers are Changing Wall Street," *Forbes ASAP* 1994, p. 29. Reprinted By Permission of *Forbes* Magazine copyright Forbes Inc., 1994.
15. Burrus, *TechnoTrends,*' p. 29.

Chapter 2:   Trends That Are Changing the Marketplace

1.   Faith Popcorn, *The Popcorn Report,* New York: HarperBusiness, 1992., p. 129.

2. Jim Snider and Terra Ziporyn, *Future Shop*, p. 268; Manning Greenberg, "Tandy Sees Changed Roles for Management in '90s," *Home Furnishings Daily*, December 18, 1989, p. 134.
3. "Mass Customization and the Changing Logistics of Manu-facturing," *Chief Executive*, November/December, 1993, p. 64. Reprinted with permission from *Chief Executive* (November/December 1993). Copyright, Chief Executive Publishing, 733 Third Avenue, 21st Floor, New York, NY 10017. All rights reserved.
4. Dave Speights, "The 25 Most Influential Trends of the Nineties," *American Marketplace* Special Report, January 1994; Business Publishers, Inc., 951 Pershing Drive, Silver Spring, MD 20910-4464, p. 8.
5. Kenneth Labich, "Class in America," *Fortune*, February 7, 1994, p. 114. Copyright 1994 Time Inc. All rights reserved.
6. Richard Winger and David Edelman, "The Art of Selling to a Segment of One," *Business Month*, January 1990, p. 79.
7. Bill Saporito, "Where the Global Action Is," *Fortune*, special issue, Autumn/Winter, p. 64. Copyright 1994 Time Inc. All rights reserved.
8. Edward Cornish, "Optimism vs. Pessimism," *The Futurist*, March/April 1994, p. 4.
9. James H. Snider, "Shopping in the Information Age," *The Futurist*, November-December 1992, p. 18.
10. Marshall Loeb, "Meet the New Consumer," special issue *Fortune*, "The Tough New Consumer," Autumn/Winter, 1993, p. 6. Copyright 1993 Time Inc. All rights reserved.
11. "EtCETERA," *American Demographics*, August 1990, p. 15. Copyright 1990. Reprinted with permission.
12. *Chain Store Age Executive*, January 1994, Lebhar-Friedman, Inc., 425 Park Avenue, New York, New York 10022.
13. Speights, "The 25 Most Influential Trends of the Nineties," p. 7.
14. *Discount Store News*, March 7, 1994, p. 8.
15. Speights, "The 25 Most Influential Trends of the Nineties," p. 7.
16. "Now you can shop while you surf the Internet," wire reports, *USA Today*, April 12, 1994, p. B-1.
17. "Home Shopping Latest Challenge for Retail Industry," The Urban Land Institute *Landuse Digest3*, Vol. 27, No. 3, March 1994, p. 1.
18. Rahul Jacob, "Beyond Quality and Value," *Fortune* Autumn/Winter 1993, p. 11. Copyright 1993 Time Inc. All rights reserved.
19. Bruce MacEvoy, "Change Leaders and the New Media," *American Demographics*, January 1994, p. 42. Copyright 1994. Reprinted with permission.
20. Barbara Clark O'Hare, "Good Deeds Are Good Business," *American Demographics*, September 1991, p. 40. Copyright 1991. Reprinted with permission.
21. Jacquelyn A. Ottman, "Message From Ecotech: Green is Good Business," Green Marketing Report. *American Marketplace*, March 24, 1994, p. 46.
22. Popcorn, *The Popcorn Report*, p. 248.
23. Ibid., p. 239.

Chapter 3:   If They Build It, These Will Come

1. John Verity and Robert D. Hoff, "The Internet--How It Will Change the Way You Do Business," *Business Week*, November 14, 1994, pp. 80-88.
2. Stephen D. Solomon, "Staking a Claim on the Internet," *Inc. Technology*, November 1994, p. 87. Reprinted with permission, *Inc.* magazine, November 1994. Copyright 1994 by Goldhirsh Group, Inc., 38 Commercial Wharf, Boston, MA 02110.
3. Ibid.

4. *Builder,* November 1994, p. 63.
5. David J. Wallace and Debra Aho Williamson, "Logging On For A Loaf Of Bread," *Advertising Age,* October 10, 1994, p. 20.
6. *Wall Street Journal,* May 13, 1994, p. B6.
7. "Interactive TV: A First Down for Chrysler," *Marketing Tools,* April/May 1994, p. 22. Copyright 1994. Reprinted with permission.
8. Jennifer Lawrence, "Will Interactive Fly on Planes?" *Advertising Age,* October 10, 1994, p. 16.
9. John Berry and Kathy Rebello, "What is an Ad in the Interactive Future?" *Business Week,* May 2, 1994, p. 103.
10. James Snider, "Consumers in the Information Age," *The Futurist,* January/February 1993, p. 16.
11. *American Demographics,* February 1994, p. 42. Copyright 1994. Reprinted with permission.
12. Bruce MacEvoy "Change Leaders and the New Media," p. 48.
13. Lee Green, "Sell A Vision," *Southwest Airlines Spirit,* October 1993, p. 44.
14. *The Numbers News,* July 1993, p. 4. Copyright 1993 American Demographics, Inc. Reprinted with permission.
15. Snider and Ziporyn, *Future Shop,* p. 87.
16. Kevin Goldman, "Industry Warned to Heed New Technology," *Wall Street Journal.* May 13, 1994, p. A12.
17. "Media Trends," *American Demographics Marketing Tools,* July 1993, excerpted from The American Forecaster Almanac, 1993 Business Edition on Disk, copyright 1993 Kim Long. Reprinted with permission.
18. Leslie Harlib, *American Demographics.* February 1994, p. 40. Copyright 1994. Reprinted with permission.
19. Nancy Coltun Webster, "Radio Tuning in to Direct Response," *Advertising Age,* October 10, 1994, p. S14.
20. Don Peppers and Martha Rogers, Ph.D., *The One to One Future.* New York: Currency Doubleday, 1993, p. 223.
21. John W. Verity, "The Internet--How it Will Change the Way You Do Business," *Business Week,* November 14, 1994, p. 84.
22. "Vernon Looks to Catalog Future," *Advertising Age,* October 10, 1994, p. S4.
23. MacEvoy, "Change Leaders and the New Media, pp. 45-48.

Chapter 4:   A Bit of This, a Byte of That

1. Alison Sprout, "Getting Mileage from a Mainframe," *Fortune,* January 10, 1994, p. 85. Copyright 1994 Time Inc. All rights reserved.
2. Thomas Forbes, "Working Toward a Greater Good," *Selling,* May 1994, p. 68. Reprinted with permission.
3. Marilyn H. Allen, "Pick Up the Pace: Technology Speeds Business," *Scottsdale Progress,* October 2, 1993, p. D1.
4. Pamela Reeves, "High-tech Process Helps Home buyers," *Scottsdale Progress Tribune,* January 15, 1994, p. E2.
5. Ibid.
6. Thomas Forbes, "How to Get Up to Speed on the Selling Superhighway," *Selling,* May 1994, p. 50. Reprinted with permission.
7. Thayer C. Taylor, "Computers Bring Quick Return," *Sales & Marketing Management,* September 1993, p. 22.

8. Elyse M. Friedman, "From the Editor," *Inc. 1994 Guide to Office Technology*, p. 10. Reprinted with permission, *Inc.* magazine. Copyright 1993 by Goldhirsh Group, Inc., 38 Commercial Wharf, Boston, MA 02110.
9. John Bielefeldt, "Sales Force Automation: Using Technol-ogy to Increase Sales," *The Stone Institute Trends & Strategies*, October 1994, p. 6. Reprinted with permission.
10. "Technophobia," *Forbes ASAP*, February 1994, p. 116. Reprinted By Permission of *Forbes* Magazine copyright Forbes Inc., 1994.
11. John Kerr, "Infomania," *Inc.*, April 1993, pp. 122-123. Reprinted with permission, *Inc.* magazine, April, 1993. Copyright 1993 by Goldhirsh Group, Inc., 38 Commercial Wharf, Boston, MA 02110.
12. Barker, *Paradigms*, p. 89.
13. *Phoenix Gazette*, December 20, 1993, p. C1.

Chapter 5:   Fishing Where the Fish Are

1. Peppers and Rogers, *The One to One Future*, p. 105
2. Dan Gutman, "Smart Tools," *Success*, May 1994, p. 45. First appeared in *Success* May 1994. Written by Dan Gutman. Reprinted with permission of *Success* magazine. Copyright ©1994 by Success Partners.
3. Dan Fost, "The Next Generation of Computer Mapping," *American Demographics*, August 1990, pp. 16-18. Copyright 1990. Reprinted with permission.
4. Kevin Goldman, "Industry Warned to Heed New Technology, p. A6.
5. John Maines, "The Box That's Challenging MTV," *American Demographics*, July 1992, p. 10. Copyright 1992. Reprinted with permission.
6. William Dunn, "Fighting the Coupon Wars," *Marketing Tools*, April/May 1994, p. 60. Copyright 1994. Reprinted with permission.
7. Peppers and Rogers, *The One to One Future*, p. 98.
8. Labich, "Class in America, p. 120.
9. Peppers and Rogers, *The One to One Future*, p. 105.
10. *American Demographics*, November 1990. Copyright 1990. Reprinted with permission.
11. Labich, "Class in America," p. 120.
12. Thomas Kobak, "How to Unmask Your Customers," *American Demographics*, July 1993, p. 53. Copyright 1993. Reprinted with permission.

Chapter 6:   The Incredible Shrinking Machine

1. James Kim, "PC Owners Flip Their Floppies for CDs," *USA Today*, April 12, 1994, p. B1.
2. Francy Blackwood, "A Bit of This, A Byte of That," *San Francisco Business*, November/December 1993, p. 35. Reprinted with permission.
3. "1994 Buyer's Guide on CD-ROM." *Builder*, April 1994, pp. 15-16.
4. "IBM Explores Vatican Link," *USA Today*, April 12, 1994, p. 4B.
5. Nikhil Huteesing, "When In Doubt, Diversify," *Forbes*, February 28, 1994, p. 105. Reprinted By Permission of *Forbes* Magazine copyright Forbes Inc., 1994.
6. Ibid.

Chapter 7:   Seeing Is Believing

1. Burrus, *TechnoTrends*, p. 339.
2. Blackwood, "A Bit of This, A Byte of That," p. 10.
3. Ibid.

4. Francy Blackwood, "High Priest of High Tech," *Selling,* September 1993, p. 21. Reprinted with permission.
5. Burrus, *TechnoTrends,* p. 339.
6. Blackwell, "A Bit of This, A Byte of That," p. 35.
7. Blackwell, "High Priest of High Tech," p. 22.
8. *Inc.,* October 1993, p. 137. Reprinted with permission, *Inc.* magazine. Copyright 1993 by Goldhirsh Group, Inc., 38 Commercial Wharf, Boston, MA 02110.
9. William J. McGuire, "Some Internal Psychological Factors Influencing Consumer Choice," *Journal of Consumer Research* 2, March 1976, pp. 302-319.
10. Dennis James, "Show and Tell," *Success.* May 1993, p. 44. First appeared in *Success* May 1993. Written by Dennis James. Reprinted with permission *Success* magazine. Copyright ©1993 by Success Partners.
11. Ibid.
12. Ibid.
13. Ibid.
14. Ibid.

Chapter 8:   E-mail or *EEEK* Mail?

1. George W. Colombo, "Get the Message: E-mail," *Selling,* April 1994, pp. 20-23. Reprinted with permission.
2. Ibid.
3. Mary Ann McNulty, "The Ticket's in the E-Mail," *CFO,* February 1994, p. 16. Reprinted with permission from the February 1994 issue of CFO, the magazine for Senior Financial Executives. Copyright 1994 CFO Publishing Corp.
4. Robert A. Mamis, "The Attention-grabbing 'Telegram'," *Inc.* June 1993, p. 47. Reprinted with permission, *Inc.* magazine, June 1993. Copyright 1993 by Goldhirsh Group, Inc., 38 Commercial Wharf, Boston, MA 02110.
5. Ibid.
6. Amy Harmon, "Mailbox Runneth Over? You Must Be Using E-Mail," *Los Angeles Times,* April 11, 1994, p. 13.
7. Jonathan Littman, "Real Estate Reinvented," *Forbes ASAP,* Spring 1994, pp. 33-35. Reprinted By Permission of *Forbes* Magazine copyright Forbes Inc., 1994.
8. Daniel R. Burk, "2000," *The Washington Lawyer,* January/ February 1994, p. 30.
9. Ibid.
10. Paul Wallich, "Wire Pirates," *Scientific American,* March 1994, p. 91.
11. Larry M. Edwards, "E-mail is Getting Stamp of Approval," *San Diego Business Journal,* March 7, 1994, p. 18.

Chapter 9:   Dialing for $$$

1. Robert A. Mamis (ed.), "Cost Cutting, Single Lines, Many Calls," *Inc.* November 1993, p. 141. Copyright 1993 by Goldhirsh Group Inc., 38 Commercial Wharf, Boston, MA 02110. Reprinted with permission.
2. Phone conversations with Harry Hart III; PR packet from company; David Volk, "This Phone Call Sponsored by Romio's Pizza," *American Demographics,* May 1993, p. 18. Copyright 1993. Reprinted with permission; and "Dialing for $$$," *Forbes,* January 3, 1994, pp. 74-75. Reprinted By Permission of *Forbes* Magazine copyright Forbes Inc., 1994.
3. "In-flight Shopping: Fliers Become Buyers," *USA Today,* April 19, 1994, p. 7B.
4. *Phoenix Gazette,* December 10, 1993, p. C5.

5. Ripley Hotch, "In Touch Through Technology," sidebar: "How Technology Can Help a Company," *Nation's Business,* January 1994, p. 35.
6. Rebecca Day, "Ringing in the New Year," *Home,* January 1994, p. 40. Reprinted with permission.
7. Ibid.
8. Ibid., p. 42.
9. David Kirkpatrick, "Intel Goes For Broke," *Fortune,* May 16, 1994, p. 66. Copyright 1994 Time Inc. All rights reserved.

Chapter 10: Welcome to Voice Mail Jail

1. *Inc.,* April 1993, p. 123.
2. William H. Davidow and Michael S. Malone, *The Virtual Corporation,* New York: HarperBusiness, 1992, p. 71.
3. Burrus, *TechnoTrends,* p. 64.
4. Rosalie Robles Crowe, "Can We Talk? Voice Mail Losing Fans," *Phoenix Gazette,* January 27, 1994, p. C6.
5. Cathy Madison, "Breaking the Voice Mail Barrier," *Selling,* December 1993, p. 57. Reprinted with permission.
6. Ibid., p. 58.
7. Peppers and Rogers, *The One to One Future,* p. 217.
8. William G. Glanagan and Toddi Gutner, "The Perils of Voice Mail," *Forbes,* January 17, 1994, p. 107.

Chapter 11: Fax to the Max

1. Patrick Marshall, "Stay in Touch," *Inc. 1994 Guide to Office Technology,* 1993, p. 60. Reprinted with permission, *Inc.* magazine Copyright 1993 by Goldhirsh Group, Inc., 38 Commercial Wharf, Boston, MA 02110.
2. Ibid.
3. *Scottsdale Progress,* October 2, 1993, p. D1.
4. David Topus, "Open Lines," *Selling,* October 1993, pp. 25-26. Reprinted with permission.

Chapter 12: World Without Wires

1. Cathy Madison, "Techno-check," *Selling,* January/February 1994, pp. 22-23. Reprinted with permission.
2. *The Yankee Group,* Vol. I, No. 5, June 1993 report.
3. *On the Air,* Vol. II, 1993, p. 3. ARDIS, 300 Knightsbridge Parkway, Lincolnshire, Ill. 60069. Reprinted with permission.
4. Ed Taylor, "McDonnell to Launch Satellite," Ed Taylor. *Scottsdale Progress Tribune,* April 15, 1994, p. B5.

Chapter 13: Home Alone?

1. Shane Tritsch, "The New Home Team," *Selling,* September 1993, p. 57. Reprinted with permission.
2. Glenn Rifkin, "Consult from Where?" *Forbes ASAP,* April 11, 1994, p. 30. Reprinted By Permission of *Forbes* Magazine copyright Forbes Inc., 1994.
3. Shane Tritsch, "The New Home Team," p. 58.
4. Ibid.
5. *LandUseDigest4,* USI--The Urban Land Institute, Volume 27, Number 4, April 1994, p. 1.

6. *Consumer Digest,* July/August 1993, p. 31.
7. Ibid.
8. Judith Schroer and Julia Lawlor, "Quake has firms turning to home work," *USA Today,* February 2, 1994, p. B2.
9. Ibid.
10. Jeffrey Young, "Vashon Statement," *Forbes ASAP,* Spring 1994, pp. 11-111. Reprinted By Permission of *Forbes* Magazine copyright Forbes Inc., 1994.
11. *Inc.,* June 1993, p. 35.
12. Shane Tritsch, "The New Home Team," p. 60.
13. Ibid.
14. Ibid., p. 61.
15. *Inc.,* June 1993, p. 35.
16. Schroer and Lawlor, "Quake has firms turning to home work," p. 2B.
17. *Inc.,* June 1993, p. 35.

Chapter 14: Trains, Planes, and Work Stations

1. Louise Driben, "Travel Fax," *Sales & Marketing Management,* June 1992, p. 139.
2. McNulty, "The Ticket's in the E-Mail," *CFO,* p. 16.
3. Phaedra Hise (researcher), *Inc.,* April 1993, p. 49.
4. John J. Xenakis, "On the Road? Phone Home," *CFO,* February 1994, Vol. 10. No. 2, p. 18. Reprinted with permission from the February 1994 issue of *CFO,* the Magazine for Senior Financial Executives. Copyright 1994 CFO Publishing Corp.

Chapter 15: Get the Picture?

1. David Topus, "Lights, Camera, Meeting!" *Selling,* November 1993, p. 24. Reprinted with permission.
2. Ibid., p. 25.
3. *Inc.,* November 1993, p. 141.
4. *Communications Industries Report,* Vol. 10, Num. 3, March 1993., p.
5. Patrick Marshall, "See Me, Hear Me," *Inc. 1994 Guide to Office Technology,* p. 60. Reprinted with permission, *Inc.* magazine. Copyright 1993 by Goldhirsh Group, Inc., 38 Commercial Wharf, Boston, MA 02110.
6. Rebecca Piirto Heather, "Future Focus Groups," *American Demographics,* January 1994, p. 6.
7. Day, "Ringing in the New Year," p. 42.
8. John Pepper and Albert G. Holzinger, "Updating Your Office Equipment," *Nation's Business,* February 1994, p. 39.
9. *Inc. Tech Guide,* 1994, p. 60.

Chapter 16: Heard Anything Yet?

1. Patrick Marshall, "Stay in Touch," p. 57.
2. Ibid., p. 59.
3. Ibid.
4. Cathy Madison, "Heard Anything Yet?" *Selling,* October 1993, pp. 78-79. Reprinted with permission.

Chapter 17: The Power of the Pen

1. Cathy Madison, "Pen Pals," *Selling,* September 1993, pp. 82-83. Reprinted with permission.
2. Ibid.

3. Pepper and Holzinger, "Updating Your Office Equipment," p. 39; and Arthur Leyenberger, "Tandy PDA/Casio Z-7000 PDA Review," *PC Laptop Computers,* April 1994, pp. 20-23.
4. Craig Patchett, "Sharp Expert Pad Review," *PC Laptop Computers,* April 1994, pp. 24-16.
5. Cathy Madison, "Techno-check," pp. 22-23.
6. Cathy Madison, "Pen Pals," pp. 82-83.

Chapter 18: Honey, They Shrunk the Computer

1. Robert A. Mamis, "Smallest Yet?" *Inc.* November 1993, p. 141.

Chapter 19: Roll the Presses

1. *What to Buy for Business,* March 1992, p. 8.
2. Cathy Madison, "Roll the Presses," *Selling,* December 1993, pp. 70-71. Reprinted with permission.

Chapter 20: Everything You Need to Know to Pick (and Pack) a Portable Phone

1. "Features-Rich Phones," *Inc.,* May 1993, special advertising section.
2. Cathy Madison, "Rules of the Road," *Selling,* August 1993, pp. 84-85. Reprinted with permission.
3. "Cellular Use and Cost Management in Business," PacTel Cellular, Walnut Creek, California.
4. *Inc.,* April 1993, p. 123.

Afterword: High-Tech vs. High-Touch

1. *What to Buy for Business,* March 1992, p. 5.

Index

A

Give the Gift
of Cutting Edge Sales Success
to Your Friends and Colleagues

ORDER FORM

YES, I want ___ copies of *TechnoSelling: How to Use Today's Technology to Sell More* at $24.95 each, plus $3 shipping per book (Texas residents please add $1.81 state sales tax per book). Canadian orders must be accompanied by a postal money order in U.S. funds. Allow 15 days for delivery.

☐ **YES**, I am interested in having Ed Callaghan speak or give a seminar on TechnoSelling to my company, association, school, or organization. Please send information.

My check or money order for $____ is enclosed.
Please charge my ☐ Visa ☐ MasterCard

Name _____ Phone _____

Organization _____

Address _____

City/State/Zip _____

Card # _____ Exp. Date _____

Signature _____

Please make your check payable and return to:
Lone Star Publishing
2300 Highland Village Road, Suite 320
Highland Village, TX 75067

Call your credit card order to: 800-896-9500
or Fax: 214-317-4091